How the
Pro-Choice Movement
Saved America

How the
Pro-Choice Movement
Saved America

Freedom, Politics, and the War on Sex

Cristina Page

BASIC
BOOKS

A Member of the Perseus Books Group

New York

Copyright © 2006 by Cristina Page

Published by Basic Books
A Member of the Perseus Books Group

All rights reserved. Printed in the United States of America. No part of this book may be
reproduced in any manner whatsoever without written permission except in the case of
brief quotations embodied in critical articles and reviews.

Design by Jane Raese
Text set in 12-point Bulmer

A CIP catalog record for this book is available from the Library of Congress.
ISBN 0-465-05489-7
ISBN-13: 978-0-465-05489-3

06 07 08 09 / 10 9 8 7 6 5 4 3 2 1

To my mother,
my husband
and my son

Contents

Preface

A FEW YEARS AGO, as I was thinking about the increasingly bitter rhetoric surrounding the abortion debate, I found myself wondering, why is there no effort to discover "common ground" between the pro-choice and pro-life movements? After all, I mused, while there were obvious differences between the movements, the shared goals were just as striking. Each side seemed determined to reduce the *need* for abortion—that was certainly clear from the hundreds of meetings I attended in the pro-choice movement. Surely, the pro-life movement would just as ardently want to cut back on the number of women who are candidates for abortions. Could there be important issues on which the two movements could happily coexist—while disagreeing on most everything else?

I'd been working in the pro-choice movement for half a dozen years when I began looking for a pro-lifer with whom I could engage in conversation on the subject. I found one: a woman about my age who worked at the largest Right to Life chapter in the country. (I work for the largest chapter of Naral Pro-Choice America.) She, like me, thought of herself as a feminist. She was a new mother, as I'd soon be. It helped that we liked one another. We began earnest, patient discussions. Perhaps encouraged by the beginnings of a friendship, we did find some common ground. In 2003, on the thirtieth anniversary of *Roe v. Wade,* we published an op-ed titled

"The Right to Agree" in the *New York Times*. In it, we staked out broad swaths of commonality: we were both against violence and violent rhetoric in the debate; we were both for policies that made being a parent easier, such as affordable child care and support for single moms; finally, and most important, we were both for measures to stop unintended pregnancies. In the editorial, we called for laws mandating that all health insurers cover contraception.

We eagerly awaited the response—we'd always thought that our discussions might lead to something ongoing, something bigger. Upon publication, response came in a torrent. Judging by letters both to me and to the *Times*' editors, most of the general public seemed thankful, if only for a momentary break from all the acrimony. One letter writer to the *Times* summarized, quite beautifully, the feelings of many: "How frequent the failures of doves and hawks, liberals and conservatives, and environmentalists and industrialists to find, or even seek, common ground? How unimaginable that the rare, shared success would come to the soul-split partisans of right to choice and right to life? 'The Right to Agree,' though framed as a call to action, is a deeply moving action in and of itself. I am in glad awe."[1]

The pro-choice movement was mildly supportive, but mostly wary, believing that I'd found in my pro-life counterpart the exception rather than the rule. But for me, the big surprise was that the pro-life movement was, well, livid.

I found the reason for its anger surprising. The point that seemed to provoke the greatest outrage among pro-lifers was the one that seemed to make the most sense: the call for better access to contraception, which to me was a no-brainer. Pro-life or pro-choice, let's not put women in a position where they need to make a decision on abortion.

I had dimly known that some people affiliated with the pro-life cause opposed contraception, but I'd assumed they were the fringe. The firestorm my coauthor experienced suggested otherwise. Her job seemed in jeopardy. Members resigned from her chapter. And there were hostile letters, a lot of them. Not all were about contraception—some people just hated the idea that a member of their movement suggested referring to abortion providers as something other than murderers—but a lot of the venom seemed directed at our stand on contraception. Among her colleagues in National Right to Life chapters, the mainstream of the pro-life movement, there seemed to be a breathtaking—and, to me, confounding—opposition to *preventing* pregnancy. What became clear to me was that if any segment of the pro-life movement supported birth control, well, *it* was the fringe.

Sadly, it quickly became apparent that our two-person brigade wasn't about to mushroom into a movement, as we'd occasionally hoped. The intensity of our personal connection petered out, perhaps inevitably. We were in different states and in very different movements. More important, as I pondered the reactions, I realized our movements also have vastly different agendas, even different values. Maybe it was just me, but I felt like my counterpart had been rebuked, especially on the contraceptive plank of our platform. And this struck me as bizarre. Why in the world would the pro-life movement, which so fervently wants to stop abortion, oppose measures that reduce the need for abortion? What is it about contraception that so irks pro-lifers? Why hadn't I, who'd been immersed in this debate, known how deep this resistance was? And what were the implications of opposing birth control?

This book is, in part, an attempt to answer those disturbing questions. In researching the answers, I came to some surprising conclusions. First, I realized that the pro-life movement is really no longer the antiabortion movement. Its agenda has lately become much broader, and to the average American it will appear much more sinister. In recent years it has turned itself into the anti–birth control movement—and, indeed, the antisex movement—whether it avows it or not. This has been largely hidden from view since the national focus is almost always on abortion—and the pro-life movement, so adept at controlling the rhetoric and symbols of this debate, certainly prefers that. Yet the pro-life movement is almost diametrically opposed to some of the cornerstones of contemporary life.

Second, it became clear to me that the pro-choice movement is actually doing a better job at what the public understands to be the pro-life agenda than pro-lifers are. In fact, it's the pro-choice movement that's largely responsible for the dramatic decline in abortion in recent years, as well as the reduction in the need for later-term abortions, a particular anathema to pro-lifers. Today, the pro-choice movement is the contraception movement too—the only one.

As a title, *How the Pro-Choice Movement Saved America* may make you uncomfortable. Even if you're pro-choice, you're likely to feel that the pro-choice movement hasn't made anything very secure. Let me explain. This book argues that we are in the midst of a culture war over sex, and the pro-choice movement is the levee, albeit eroding, that has kept a growing wave of pro-life fundamentalism from washing over our way of life. Pro-lifers are often cast as godly, righteous, "moral." Their language is emotional, religious, almost utopian, and frequently they use it to suggest that the world is going to hell in a handbasket, often because of abortion and, lately, contraception. The pro-choice movement is usually relegated to the role of the steely-eyed realist, the heartless pragmatist who often appears on TV as the inscrutable scientist. But the more I thought about it, the clearer it seemed to me that the pro-choice movement is not just a dispassionate explainer. We are defending a way of life, one that we helped usher in more than a quarter of a century ago as the contraception revolution got under way. We are not simply sticking up for the right to an abortion. We are taking a stand on sex.

Pro-lifers tend to believe, whether they say it out loud or not, that sex should be for the sole purpose of producing a baby. Pro-choicers accept sex as something that people do for intimacy and for pleasure. And because of that, they work for wider use of contraception. More than that, pro-choicers celebrate its power in all of our lives, the power to choose when and if we want to have a family (and to decide, once we've begun one, how large it should be). And this, let's face it, is in step with the way Americans live. The average American woman spends more than thirty years of her life using artificial means to control her reproductive ability. Even 85 percent of Catholic women, in defiance of Church doctrine, believe in artificial birth control (and most practice it as well). The pro-choice side rejoices in every societal advance that has come from this simple control, which is nothing short of a flowering of equality in school, at work, and at home.

This book is, in part, about the hidden anticontraception agenda of the pro-life movement. But it is also about the implications of that stance. If you read the Web sites, speeches, and testimony of pro-life leaders, as I have, it is difficult to escape the view that what they most pine for is a world in which the role of women is simple and straightforward. We stay home to raise children. This is a bedrock pro-life ideal. In the pro-choice world, which also happens to be the world we actually live in, women can be lawyers, doctors, pilots, whatever, as well as mothers. Women, taking advantage of changes wrought by the pro-choice movement, go to college in greater numbers than men, earn as much, decide elections. Generations of children have prospered from better-educated, worldlier, more independent, and wealthier mothers. The expanded lives women enjoy have in turn allowed a generation of men to be better and more involved fathers, lovers, friends, and colleagues. (Some of the greatest damage to the pro-choice cause comes in the form of friendly fire, from those who cast this issue as one that exclusively concerns women.)

The pro-choice movement may have ceded much of the rhetorical advantage to the pro-lifers (the made-up term *partial-birth abortion* just sounds so much more ominous than *late-term abortion,* which is the medical term), but it's the pro-choice movement that has helped construct and that now defends our dearest values, those that Americans largely identify as their own. We value control over our destinies, independence, equality. These are pro-choice values, and they have come to best represent the values of our culture. The way to understand the title of this book is as a two-sided coin. How the pro-choice movement saved America is the side that celebrates our accomplishments, our values; the other side is how the pro-life movement is trying to undo all those gains, particularly for women, that we now take for granted.

How the
Pro-Choice Movement
Saved America

chapter one

Rights in Jeopardy

January 2004: A woman is released from the emergency room. She's just been raped. After treatment, she is given a prescription for emergency contraception (EC) to prevent her from getting pregnant by the attacker. This is standard procedure. EC is just two birth control pills, but taken up to seventy-two hours after sex it is effective at averting a pregnancy. A friend takes her to an Eckerd pharmacy in Denton, Texas, to fill the prescription. Though the pharmacist had declined five or six times in the past to fill such prescriptions, this is the first time a rape victim has requested the medication. The pharmacist goes to the back room, prays, and calls his pastor before deciding not to fill the prescription. The two other pharmacists on duty decline to fill the prescription as well.[1] The friend of the rape victim explains, "I had been watching my friend, her emotional state going down and down and down. And I knew I was going to have to . . . say, 'Sorry, you know, morally they say you're wrong.'"[2]

March 2004: Julee Lacey, a thirty-two-year-old first grade teacher and mother of two, is told by her local CVS pharmacist, "I'm sorry, but I personally do not believe in birth control, so I will not fill your prescription." *Lacey's husband and the assistant manager of CVS cannot persuade the pharmacist to change her mind.* "*I think my doctor should make these decisions,*" *Mrs. Lacey says.* "*If they're going to decide not to do birth control pills, where are they going to draw the line? A lot of doctors don't believe in transplants,*" *she adds.* "*Where will this go?*"[3]

July 2004: Idalia Moran attempts to fill her prescription for birth control pills at a Medicine Shoppe pharmacy in Fabens, Texas. The pharmacist, after having recently listened to a radio program that claimed birth control pills cause abortions, tells Moran he will not fill her prescription because it is against his religion. Moran then drives thirty-three miles to El Paso, the next nearest pharmacy willing to fill her prescription for standard birth control pills.[4]

September 2004: On a Saturday night, twenty-one-year-old single mother Suzanne Richards tries to fill a prescription for emergency contraception at the drive-through Brooks pharmacy in Laconia, New Hampshire. The pharmacist declines to fill her doctor's prescription and tells her, "*I believe this will end the fertilization of the egg and this conception was your choice.*" *Richards pulls her car over in the parking lot and cries. She returns to the pharmacy later that night with her father; the pharmacist again refuses to fill the prescription and will not tell her where she can get it filled. Richards explains,* "*He said I was irresponsible. Well, I think it's irresponsible to have kids you can't take care of and raise.*"[5]

MOST OF US HAVE LONG ACCEPTED the terms of one of the central debates of American culture, the debate over abortion. The first thing that we accept is what it's about, which is supposed to be abortion. On one side, a movement that cleverly calls itself pro-life (suggesting that its opponents must be, needless to say, pro-death) says it opposes the right to abortion. On the other side, a movement that less cleverly calls itself pro-choice supports the right to abortion.

But when you take a closer look, these simple views of what the two sides stand for hardly begin to describe what lately is, and really always has been, at the heart of this growing American conflict. These movements encompass far more; abortion isn't the keystone issue anymore. It's birth control and, more to the point, Americans' sex lives. Abortion has been the attention-getting focus, the easy divider, a convenient way to rally troops, but the pro-choice and pro-life movements are essentially about competing ways of life. Indeed, to be pro-life today means to be inside a movement that finds fault with every kind of birth control, from the Pill, which revolutionized women's (and men's) lives, to the condom, which in our era is the last stand against the most virulent sexually transmitted diseases (STDs). To be pro-life means to favor abstinence until marriage, in part because they believe that sex is supposed to be for one purpose only: to procreate.

Those vigilante acts of obstruction-by-pharmacist, which grow in frequency each year, appear on the surface independent from one another. And as such, they seem a little kooky, a little outrageous. Who is this wayward pharmacist defying a doctor's order? Who, because of his own dubious religious notions, takes a patient's medical destiny in his own hands? But these are not random acts. Behind each are the force and rhetoric of the pro-life move-ment, taken directly from their newsletters and downloaded off their Web sites.

And there's more than just rhetoric involved. Every time these acts have been challenged (who knows how many times they have not been), the pro-life movement has responded with legislation to protect, lawyers to defend, and spokespeople to spin for the phar-macists who have denied women the chance to prevent pregnancy. Why, one might ask, would the pro-life movement invest itself in such extreme acts, not against abortion but against birth control? If the movement's only aim is to stop abortions—and stop them by any means—then why attack people who say they don't want to get pregnant? If you don't want people to have abortions, then why not help them prevent unwanted pregnancies? After all, studies have shown that the use of contraception reduces the probability of hav-ing an abortion by 85 percent.[6] Why would those so adamantly against abortion seem to hamper practical, simple, and safe at-tempts to actually prevent abortions? It turns out that none of the women named above—Julee, Suzanne, Idalia—wanted to have an abortion. (There's a good chance some of them are even pro-life.) Suzanne went back to the pharmacy with her father, in the hopes of heading off an abortion. Julee brought in her husband and even in-volved the store manager to convince the pharmacist to allow her to prevent pregnancy. Another woman summoned the police to inter-vene on her behalf when a pharmacist refused to even release her prescription to be filled elsewhere. No one could do anything.

It seems no coincidence that these women, instinctively, brought in strong authority figures, and men, to intervene for them. Their authority as women was being challenged, and they knew it.

Weren't the pharmacists treating each as an immoral, loose woman deserving of the consequences of what they perceived as inappropriate, simply-for-pleasure sex? In the pharmacists' eyes, these women had made a mistake, a moral mistake, and the pharmacists chose to punish them for it. Even the trauma of rape didn't manage to make a woman a special case, not in the eyes of the pharmacist. She waited in the parking lot while the pharmacist mused over his own feelings, then turned her away without the medication the emergency room prescribed.

The result of these events was that each woman became infinitely more likely to have an abortion. Indeed, it's one of the profound ironies of the pro-life movement that its work hasn't led to fewer abortions. Just the opposite. Studies of states that have enacted pro-life laws show what these laws succeed at most is increasing the number of later-term abortions. As for the nation as a whole, it witnessed its most dramatic decline in abortion rates during the presidency of Bill Clinton, our first pro-choice president. In 1990, just two years before Clinton took office, the number of abortions in the United States was at one of the highest levels ever. By the end of Clinton's second term, the abortion rate had dropped to the lowest in a quarter of a century.[7]

One would think that for those who wish to end abortion, this discrepancy would lead to self-reflection, perhaps even a willingness to look more closely at the policies that led to the effects they claim to seek. But in the face of evidence that allowing women unfettered access to birth control leads to fewer abortions, the pro-life movement has intensified its campaigns and rhetoric against birth control. And the real, underlying reason is that to allow birth control would mean tolerating a lifestyle that allows people to enjoy sex outside of marriage and parenthood. Contraception, which for many is the era's most liberating technology, is to pro-lifers an evil just like abortion. In fact, in the literature of the contemporary pro-life movement, often no distinction is made. Reducing abortions has, in a sense, become problematic for them. The problem is that it means favoring the use of contraception, and, in effect, endorsing a way of life, and a view of sex, that they oppose perhaps even more strongly than they oppose abortion. So whereas banning abortion gets the headlines, it's banning contraception that is increasingly creeping into the pro-life agenda. To pro-lifers, they are, in fact, two avenues to accomplish one thing: end the lifestyle in which people have sex just for pleasure.

And so, to return to the vigilante pharmacists and their "moral" decision to obstruct the contraceptive decisions of others, it would seem, on the face of it, that they are promoting unwanted pregnancies and risking more abortions, just the ends these radical pharmacists claim they oppose. Yet they are generally lauded within the pro-life movement as principled people of good faith and true values—not because they stopped an abortion (they may well have had the opposite effect) but, and this is the only conclusion possible, because they advanced the new anti–birth control agenda that increasingly seems at the heart of the pro-life movement.

Today, 42 million American women (that's 7 in 10 women of reproductive age) are sexually active and do not want to become pregnant—but could become pregnant if they or their partners fail to use a contraceptive method.[8] In fact, only 5 percent of women aged 15–44 in the United States are not using any contraceptive method during sex.[9] And from this 5 percent come nearly 50 percent of the nation's abortions.[10] All available and accepted research leads to one conclusion: proper use of and access to contraception results in a dramatic decline in abortion. Yet few Americans would believe that some of the fiercest pro-life/pro-choice conflicts raging in state legislatures and in Congress right now are over the right to use birth control. But just look at the mission statement of the nation's largest pro-life educational organization, the American Life League (A.L.L.): "A.L.L. denies the moral acceptability of artificial birth control and encourages each individual to trust in God, to surrender to His will, and to be predisposed to welcoming children."[11] In the volumes of writing A.L.L. publishes on the subject of birth control they even equate contraception with genocide.[12] Sound extreme? Doesn't resemble the thoughts of that pro-life cousin or neighbor you've had the quiet disagreements with? That's because the pro-lifer in your life probably doesn't agree with it either. It's very likely your pro-life cousin or neighbor also doesn't know that the organizations she has happily sent donations off to are spearheading initiatives that are leading to more abortions.

For example, since 2001 the Right to Life movement has responded to a wave of pharmacists' refusals to fill birth control prescriptions with one favorite tactic. It has moved aggressively to welcome them as acts of "conscience." The movement has helped pass laws in South Dakota, Arkansas, and Mississippi allowing pharmacists to refuse on moral or religious grounds to fill birth control prescriptions without fear of being fired or sued for damages. In nineteen states, they've moved to protect *anyone* who might like to stand in the way of a woman getting birth control.[13] This conceivably could include righteous cashiers who'll refuse to ring up your prescription. As Elizabeth Graham, director of the Texas Right to Life Committee in Houston, explained, "Texas

Right to Life supports conscience laws that would include not only allowing pharmacists but all healthcare workers from providing medicine to which they are morally opposed."[14] Kelly Copeland, director of the Southern Arizona Life Team, supported her state's "right of refusal" legislation. The *Arizona Daily Star* explained that Copeland believed the legislation would be a "positive solution" for physicians and pharmacists who are currently "forced to pre-scribe and dispense birth control against their moral beliefs."[15] Americans United for Life offers model legislation on their Web site "to protect *any individual,* including nurses' aides, pharma-cists, students, and others who may be in the situation of having to participate in a health care service to which he or she conscien-tiously objects, or risk disciplinary action or liability for his or her failure to participate."[16]

Medicine has in recent years proudly moved to an evidence-based model defined as "the conscientious, explicit and judicious use of current best evidence in making decisions about the care of individual patients."[17] The Right to Life movement would clearly like to go in another direction, to a no-exceptions, evidence-free ap-proach based on a set of ever-changing "beliefs." They call it "con-science"-based medicine. The conscience, it should be noted, isn't that of the woman patient, who doesn't really factor into this hand-wringing, but that of the immaculate pharmacist, or nurse, or, per-haps, the cashier at your local Wal-Mart.

The pro-life movement is well financed, active, and is often the only opponent of the many attempts to allow American women greater access to birth control. The headquarters of the National Right to Life Committee includes in its mission statement a dis-claimer saying it does "not have a position on issues such as contraception."[18] But that's a notable exception—and a convenient cover—to the rest of the nation's pro-life groups, including many of National Right to Life's state chapters, which are actively involved in anti–birth control campaigns. It's worth pausing for an instant to consider the logic of this position. You'd think that people who are profoundly and sincerely against abortion would do everything in their power, including promoting birth control, to prevent unwanted pregnancies. But there is not one pro-life group in the United States that supports the use of birth control. Shouldn't the American people, pro-lifers included, wonder why, if a group's aim is to end abortion, spreading the contraceptive message isn't a *central* part of its mission? Imagine the outrage if the National Cancer Institute's strategy was to discourage the use of the most successful cancer preventatives, and instead tried to ban them. What if it only encouraged people to abstain from cancer-causing behaviors and environments and then when they got cancer called it God's will?

In 1998, pro-life operatives were behind the defeat of federal legislation to require health insurance companies to pay for contraceptives. Even a predictable opponent of the plan, the insurance industry, declined to testify against the federal contraceptive-coverage bill. The Pro-Life Caucus of Congress, however, led a full-on assault.[19] Congressman Jim McDermott (D-WA), who witnessed the proceedings, commented on the pro-life Republicans' role in the defeat of the legislation:

> This is a party that is not content with trying to roll back abortion rights. It is fighting on several fronts against contraception. Just last week the Republican leadership in the House, under pressure from the right, killed a measure that would have required federal health

plans that cover prescription drugs to cover the cost of contraceptives. No one seemed to think it was crazy to have abortion foes opposing a measure that would reduce the need for abortions. They could not grasp that.[20]

Nor, apparently, could they grasp why a woman ought to be allowed emergency contraception after a brutal sexual attack. The pro-life movement is also the only opponent of legislation to provide pregnancy prevention to rape victims. The Florida, Hawaii, Massachusetts, and Louisiana state affiliates of National Right to Life, as well as pro-life groups in Colorado and Wisconsin, all fought against legislation to make emergency contraception—which, don't forget, is nothing more than a higher dose of birth control pills—available to rape victims.[21]

Over the past decade we have witnessed the brilliance of the pro-life movement in defining terms. More clever still is that they sometimes invent science to fit their cause. They have become adept at "medicalizing" their religious or cultural arguments so that they appear to be factual and credible. One of their most recognized campaigns was with "partial-birth abortion," a gruesome term that didn't exist before they invented it. With it, they managed to convince the public that full-term, healthy babies were being aborted moments before birth. Implied in this message was the notion that many women, having endured eight months of pregnancy, finally decided to "choose." Have you ever met a woman in her eighth month of pregnancy for whom the disappearance of her fetus wasn't also accompanied by a tragic story—typically one of a very much wanted but unviable pregnancy?

Inherent in the partial-birth-abortion message is an awesome contempt for women and the medical realities, and sometimes tragedies, of pregnancy. Lost in the debate is that less than two-tenths of 1 percent of all abortions use the procedure that pro-lifers describe.[22] And third-trimester abortion is already illegal in most of the United States except to save a woman's life or protect her health. In those cases, doctors are required to use the best methods available. Had one abortion technique been banned, doctors would have been required to use another, possibly less safe, method in order to treat patients experiencing grave pregnancy problems in the third trimester. The "partial-birth abortion" ban would not have ended any of the latest abortions, which is what the pro-life movement led the public to believe.

The campaign did succeed, however, in convincing the public that something that isn't a problem is. Pro-lifers presented these bans as the solution the public very much wanted—ending perceived gruesome, unnecessary, late-term abortions had by women with no conscience, performed by doctors motivated by greed (never patient need). Instead, the bans did something the public didn't want at all—the legislation was so broadly written it banned all abortions, including those used to rescue women from physical danger, anytime after twelve weeks of pregnancy. And although, so far, the partial-birth-abortion bans have been held unconstitutional by the courts, they have been, in more important ways, a huge success for the pro-life movement. For pro-lifers, it was an intoxicating campaign. They invented an issue, basked in the public's favor, raised unprecedented amounts of money, and, most important, didn't suffer any consequences for masquerading as more knowledgeable in medicine than the whole of the medical establishment. Rather than fight science, they became science—but without evidence, expertise, or transparent aims. They played doctors on TV, and the public accepted their version of it.

This is not the first or only time the pro-lifers have invented a problem, presented phony "evidence," and provoked the true experts to step forth to set the record straight. Take, for example, "post-abortion stress syndrome." This is a disorder, they claim, that affects women who have had abortions and is characterized by a set of symptoms including guilt, regret, remorse, shame, lowered self-esteem, insomnia, nightmares, flashbacks, anniversary reactions, hostility (even hatred) toward men, sexual dysfunction, crying, despair, depression, alcohol or drug use that they say leads to sexual promiscuity, suicide attempts, and a "numbing and coldness" in place of "more normal warmth and maternal tenderness."[23] Because pro-life groups were increasingly presenting these unfounded claims as fact, the American Psychological Association (APA), the largest association of psychologists worldwide, assembled an expert panel to study the issue.

The APA discovered that actual research on the subject revealed the exact opposite of what the pro-lifers claim. One study followed 360 adolescents for two years after they had been interviewed when seeking a pregnancy test. The study included girls who thought they might be pregnant but turned out not to be, some who were pregnant and carried to term, and some who were pregnant and then aborted the pregnancy. The researchers found that

> the adolescents who chose abortion showed significant drops in anxiety and significant increases in self esteem and internal control in the period immediately following the abortion to two years later. They appeared to be functioning as well as, *or even better than*, adolescents who turned out not to be pregnant or had carried to term. They were also most likely to have higher economic well-being;

most likely to be in high school (and performing at grade level) or to have graduated; and less likely to have a subsequent pregnancy.[24]

The panel concluded that, despite the pro-life movement's hopeful assertions, legal abortion simply didn't cause psychological trauma, despite the obvious stresses involved in an unwanted pregnancy. The panel discovered that after an abortion, emotions are complicated, positive, and, yes, negative, but not long lasting. "The time of greatest stress is before the abortion," the panel concluded. Based on a review of the research, the American Psychological Association recommended: "Access to legal abortion to terminate an unwanted pregnancy is vital to safeguard both the physical and mental health of women. Research indicates that abortion does not generally have a negative impact on either women's physical or mental health." The *experts* in the field found that abortion had no detrimental effect on women's mental health, and they wound up recommending access to abortion in order to *ensure* women's mental health. What could hurt women psychologically? "A forced, unwanted pregnancy . . . could place women's health and well-being at risk," the panel said.[25]

Every decision related to an unintended pregnancy comes with its range of emotions, and, yes, all decisions, including abortion, are traumatic for some women. Postpartum depression is, unlike postabortion stress syndrome, a known disorder documented by verifiable research and accepted by every medical group that has considered it. Indeed, giving up a baby for adoption can cause extreme emotional trauma for a woman too, in some cases exponentially more than other options. To stoke emotion that stems from placing a baby for adoption, which is what pro-lifers do with the women who experience grief after abortion, would be mean, vindictive. Yet more than a hundred pro-life groups market post-abortion stress syndrome. Not because there is conclusive evidence of it, but because they don't play by the rules of evidence. They understand that if the majority of the public believes something, it's as good as true. If it is said loud enough for long enough that women are traumatized by abortion, women just might start to feel ashamed after abortion—in which case, of course, pro-life advocates will be there to empathize with them.

Having succeeded in tailoring medicine to fit their ideology, the pro-life movement is now attempting a similar trick with birth control. The public, pro-life and pro-choice alike, supports the use of birth control. Even practicing Catholics, followers of the only religion opposed to every birth control method, overwhelmingly favor (and practice) birth control. When polled, 85 percent of U.S. Catholics said they believe that *they should be allowed to practice artificial means of birth control.*[26] From the American public's point of view, this is *the* common ground issue: everyone uses birth control, and we're all in favor of it, especially because it prevents the need for abortion. So in order for pro-life groups to advance in their anti–birth control campaigns, birth control must become something different. Pro-lifers therefore now attempt to reclassify the most common contraceptive methods as abortion. Having by and large won the abortion debate, they have broadened the definition of abortion to include the Pill, the shot, the patch, the ring, the IUD.

Calling run-of-the-mill contraception an abortion is a breathtaking bit of misinformation. But it's working. Pro-lifers have defeated efforts intended to make birth control available while, and this is the magic, appearing to not be against birth control (only against abortion). And by doing so they camouflage an agenda that is completely out of step with the lifestyle that most Americans embrace and enjoy.

Take, for example, the campaigns started in the nineties (which continue today) to get health insurance companies to cover contraception. In 1990, the birth control pill had been around for more than thirty years. Even though 82 percent of all American women born since 1945 have used the Pill,[27] it, along with all other contraceptives, was still not included in most insurance plans. Consequently, American women were still paying for contraception out of pocket, amounting to 68 percent more in health care expenses than men.[28] In 1996, the Federal Drug Administration (FDA) approved the erection drug Viagra. Viagra obviously had no "health care" or "prevention" functions, yet it took just less than two months for half of all prescriptions of Viagra to be covered by health insurers.[29]

The irony, and the kick in the face, was not lost on the pro-choice movement. Suddenly, its efforts to get birth control covered were infused with new energy. The public joined in with near consensus in favor of birth control coverage. And pro-life groups faced for the first time the prospect of widespread access to contraception becoming the norm. This posed an enormous threat to their broader agenda. Still, it would be too damaging for pro-lifers to admit they oppose birth control. So in a calculating move with far-reaching consequences, they changed the debate. They turned it into something they could be against. Suddenly, contraception became abortion.

In 2004, the Ohio legislature considered a bill to make insurers cover birth control. Paula Westwood, executive director of Right to Life of Greater Cincinnati, argued against the bill, claiming that "contraception isn't medically necessary." Then she added, "Some people define contraceptives very broadly to include the RU486 abortion drug."[30] But no one was suggesting that RU-486, which is, in fact, an abortion method, is contraception except Paula Westwood. The proposed bill was clear. Ohio's contraceptive legislation did not propose to cover RU-486 or any other abortion method. (Nor, by the way, did contraceptive-coverage bills in any other state.) Yet, to oppose these bills, right-to-lifers systematically blurred the lines between contraception and abortion. Judith Aungst, vice president of Delaware Right to Life, fought that state's contraceptive legislation, saying, "Fertility is not a disease but a function of a woman's normal, healthy reproductive organs," which is the standard opening in these appeals. Then, she added, "Contraceptives and abortifacients interfere with this." To her, a contraceptive, something that prevents a pregnancy, and an abortifacient, something that ends a pregnancy, are to be treated as one and the same. Mike Jacobs, of the Delaware Life political action committee, furthered the cleverly constructed argument by choosing to not even mention contraception. "The problem [with contraceptive coverage] is, if you're a member of an insurance company, then your premiums are paying for *someone else's abortion* and we don't feel that's quite right."[31]

These bills, it's worth underscoring, had nothing to do with abortion. They covered the Pill, the diaphragm, the Depo-Provera shot, and the IUD. The weirdest aspect of the pro-life argument was that most health insurers already willingly paid for actual abortions. Indeed, women had a much greater chance of having an abortion bill footed by an insurer than a bill for a birth control pill. Yet claiming these contraceptive-coverage bills covered abortion—a meaningless bit of doublespeak—became the soundtrack for the pro-life campaign. It was the strategy the movement used to successfully prevent women from getting health insurance coverage of the birth control methods they already used.

Soon one pro-life group after the next rose up against efforts to make contraception more available. Nevada Right to Life falsely claimed its state legislation covered abortions too.[32] The legislation did not. In 2003, Illinois Right to Life also charged that its state's contraceptive-coverage bill would require insurers to pay for abortions even though the bill stated plainly, "Nothing in this section shall be construed to require an insurance company to cover services related to an abortion."[33] Even when the bill passed, Illinois Right to Life continued to describe the birth control bill as "pro-abortion," and the legislative round-up section of their Web site still claims that it is "legislation which forces insurance coverage of abortificients [*sic*]."[34] Using the same technique, Oregon Right to Life succeeded in defeating its state's contraceptive-coverage legislation.[35] The American Life League called for pro-life groups and individuals around the country to "please tell your state lawmakers to ignore bogus arguments about 'gender equity' and 'fairness' and urge them to vote against these proposals. You might also remind them that many forms of birth control, including Depo-Provera, the IUD and the Pill, can cause early abortion."[36]

The pro-life side didn't always get away with the verbal trickery. In a few instances, the media exposed the pro-life opposition to these bills, pointing out that the pro-lifers were also the originators of these fabrications and distortions. An editorial in the *Capital Times,* for example, explained that Wisconsin's contraceptive legislation "would provide coverage for five FDA-approved prescription contraceptives and would not provide coverage for

RU-486"—an abortion method. "Nevertheless, the bill has drawn the opposition of the state's largest anti-abortion group, Wisconsin Right to Life, as well as Pro-Life Wisconsin." The editors, mystified by the pro-life opposition, added, "And yet, it is access to safe, affordable birth control that allows women to plan their families and avoid the possibility of abortion."[37] A 2001 op-ed in St. Louis, Missouri's *Riverfront Times* explained how Sam Lee, head of Campaign Life Missouri, used abortion as a cover to successfully ban state funding for contraceptive services to more than 30,000 poor women.

> The saga lays bare the hypocrisy of the self-proclaimed pro-lifers. The warriors for the unborn aren't so committed to life that they'd compromise their own sense of morality . . . even if it means preventing the need for abortion in the first place. . . . Lee launched his assault on family-planning programs, cleverly couched as nothing more than an effort to keep public funds from being used to kill the unborn. Painfully aware of widespread public support for family planning, Lee and his cohorts have always hid behind the anti-abortion fig leaf in their attacks.[38]

Even Catholic groups, who openly admit they're against all forms of birth control, didn't oppose contraceptive-coverage bills as vociferously as the pro-life movement. The Catholic establishment didn't fight to deny *all* women the right to coverage, which is what the pro-life groups did. The Catholics complained that they didn't want their organizations to be forced to provide contraceptive coverage to their employees. They also didn't try to argue that it was abortion that was being covered. Pro-choice groups have successfully fought through contraceptive-coverage bills in many states, yet today still fewer than half have laws mandating that contraception be as available to women as Viagra now is to men.[39]

The right-to-life movement's campaign against birth control is disciplined—witness the uniform messages in state after state—and enforced. In April 2002, the *Cincinnati Enquirer* reported in an article titled "Right to Life Adds Pill to List" that "to receive the endorsement of the powerful Northern Kentucky Right to Life, candidates must now state that they think the use of the standard birth control pill—not just the morning after pill—constitutes abortion." Apparently, even some pro-lifers thought this was a little crazy. A pro-life elected official, Barb Black, refused to return the organization's candidate questionnaire, explaining, "To get the endorsement of Northern Kentucky Right to Life, you had to have been willing to grit your teeth, shut your eyes, turn off your brain and mark 'yes.'" The same affiliate of National Right to Life also attempted to ban all artificial birth control—meaning anything but the rhythm method—in the local health district.[40] (It didn't want any method available to *anyone.*) Under the proposed resolution, every type of artificial birth control would be construed as "pro-abortion." Another affiliate, Texas Right to Life, indicated in their 2004–2005 state legislature questionnaire that they would not endorse any candidate who supported access to emergency contraception, even to provide it to rape victims hoping to not become impregnated by a rapist.[41]

The right-to-life movement has been particularly energetic in spreading its message online, where it seems to have, if anything, less compunction about mixing fact and fiction. Sometimes this confusing mix appears to be a simple mistake. Other times, it clearly is part of a strategy calculated to convert people to the cause. When it comes to converting, there are probably few groups more resourceful or cunning than the pro-life movement. For example, do you think www.prochoice.com is a pro-choice site? Think again. It's a pro-life site. Likewise, www.birthcontrol.org turns out to be an anticontraception Web site that exclusively promotes the use of "natural family planning."[42] The trick, as always, is to persuade the visitor that contraception and abortion are really one and the same. For instance, a recent visit to the Illinois Federation for Right to Life's Web site offers seventy-seven news articles under the category "Chemical Abortion." But sixty-four of them—that's an impressive 83 percent—are actually about what most Americans consider contraception. (The remaining thirteen news stories in the section were about abortion methods.)[43] The Iowa Right to Life Committee lists on its Web site under its "glossary of abortifacients" the IUD, Norplant, Implanon, and Depo-Provera, all of which it apparently wants to ban.[44] (Until I called to see if they were serious, Wisconsin Right to Life's Web site proclaimed that the diaphragm and spermicides cause abortions too. After my inquiry they removed that claim.)[45]

From the seemingly mainstream to the scariest and extreme pro-life groups, the anti–birth control message is blended seamlessly with their so-called mission against abortion. Missionaries to the Preborn offers advice to "engaged and newlywed couples." On their Web site, they call one section "Everything you never wanted to know about birth control." In it appears a table titled "Calculated Annual Infant Homicides of Unborn Babies in the USA." From the table, the claim is clear: the Pill, IUD, Depo-Provera, and Norplant cause between 5 million and 20 million "infant homicides" each year.[46] Not surprisingly, Army of God, a pro-life organization that lists those who murder abortion providers as "heroes,"[47] also classifies birth control as an abortion method.[48] It-makes one wonder if future Army of God "heroes" might include those who murder physicians for writing prescriptions for the Pill. In a section chillingly called "Birth Control Is Evil," the Army of God Web site states boldly, almost threateningly, "Birth control is evil and a sin. Birth control is anti-baby and anti-child. . . . Why would you stop your own child from being conceived or born? What kind of human being are you?"[49]

THE PRO-LIFE MOVEMENT MAY, through repetition, hope to convince us that contraception is abortion. What are the facts? Is there really no difference between abortion and contraception? To understand the answer, we must start with a quick explanation of pregnancy, what it is and when it begins. According to the American College of Obstetricians and Gynecologists[50] and the National Institutes of Health (NIH),[51] pregnancy begins when a fertilized egg implants in the womb. Until it affixes to the woman's womb a fertilized egg cannot receive nutrients from the woman's body, which is essential for survival. Implantation is also the first moment at which a pregnancy can be determined; no test can establish that an egg has been fertilized. On this one point, science, medicine, and the law agree: implantation is the moment at which pregnancy starts. Only the dissenting pro-life movement dismisses this definition. It, instead, would like pregnancy to start at the unknowable moment the sperm fertilizes the egg. Once sperm meets egg, the pro-life movement considers any effort to prevent the egg from implanting in the womb an abortion. This is one of the arguments they offer up as justification for the campaigns to keep women from using birth control. (Other arguments include: sex is exclusively a procreative act, and conception is God's will.) To make this justification work, pro-lifers claim that most birth control methods prevent fertilized eggs from implanting in the womb, which to them—though not to medical science—is an abortion. This, though, is another misconception. Even if we accept their proposition that fertilization commences a pregnancy, their argument is still untenable. They'd like us to take the next step and believe that contraception stops a fertilized egg from implanting. But again, science doesn't support that claim. There just is no evidence that birth control methods do what pro-life groups would like them to do.

In 1999, prompted in part by the growing efforts of pro-life groups to define birth control as abortion, the *American Journal of Obstetrics and Gynecology* reviewed the available research on "the mechanism of action" of contraceptive methods that so dismay pro-lifers.[52] The authors take up the pro-life concerns directly: "Recently, some special interest groups have claimed, without providing any scientific rationale, that some methods of contraception may have an abortifacient effect." After reviewing the literature, the authors conclude that hormonal contraceptive methods (oral contraceptives, the patch, the ring, the shot) cause a number of changes in a woman's body that prevent pregnancy. Primarily, what they do is prevent ovulation. In other words, a woman who takes the Pill will in almost all instances not release an egg. No egg, no chance of pregnancy. The secondary way these contraceptives function, the authors report, is by preventing fertilization. So on the very slim chance that a woman using a hormonal method does produce an egg, another mechanism of action kicks in. Hormonal contraceptives also thicken the mucous lining of women's reproductive organs, which hampers the ability of the sperm to even get to the egg. This is what *is* known about how hormonal birth control works.

What gets pro-lifers so worked up is their persistent belief that a fertilized egg can be stopped from implanting in the womb. We know hormonal contraceptives stop fertilization. What if, through some extraordinary, unknown, and seemingly unknowable process, an egg got fertilized? The researchers consider the question and report, "No direct evidence exists showing that implantation is prevented by progestin-only methods," and they add that "the evidence does not support the theory that the usual mechanism of action of IUDs is destruction of fertilized ova in the uterus." After reviewing all the research available on the modes of action of all contraceptives in question, the authors summarize their report by explaining that (1) hormonal methods work primarily by inhibiting ovulation and through changes in cervical mucus, and (2) the IUD works through the prevention of fertilization. "All of these methods, directly or indirectly, have effects on the endometrium [the lining of the uterus] that might prevent implantation of a fertilized ovum," the researchers acknowledge. But they quickly point out, "So far, no scientific evidence has been published supporting this possibility." In other words, there's no evidence that any birth control method prevents a fertilized egg from attaching to the womb, even though that mechanism of action is the basis for the pro-life claims.

What's most striking about all this information is that it really should be a relief to pro-lifers. Birth control doesn't have any effect on the egg once it is fertilized. The primary and secondary ways in which these methods work should be completely acceptable to them.

In fact, though, they've taken just the opposite stance. Their argument usually goes like this: "We can't really know for sure that in some cases, however rare, a fertilized egg isn't kept from fulfilling its God-decreed destiny of implanting in the womb. And the dutiful scientist, limited by the research facts, must acknowledge that although no evidence suggests that such a thing happens, it's impossible to rule it out. So there!" It can't be ruled out. You can't prove a negative.

The pro-life movement's stance is like deriding gravity as a hypothesis. Yes, the last ten times you dropped that spoon, it crashed down on the table. But what about the eleventh time? Or the eleven hundredth? Or the eleven millionth? Pro-life campaigns are not interested in scientific or medical examination of facts; their stance against birth control is based largely on wishful thinking. Indeed, because of a slim hypothetical chance, the pro-life movement has successfully opposed legislation that would have provided millions of women access to effective birth control methods.

Even some pro-life physicians, sparked by the recurring actions by the pro-life movement against birth control, stepped into the fray. In 1998, twenty-two pro-life ob-gyns published an analysis titled *Birth Control Pills: Contraceptive or Abortifacients?* and four of these pro-life physicians followed up with a more detailed paper on hormonal contraceptives in general. The pro-life doctors weighed in because they were concerned that the theory that birth control is an abortion is getting the status "scientific fact" among their brethren. So what did these pro-life physicians conclude? They state it as plainly as they can: "The 'hormonal contraception is abortifacient' theory is not established scientific fact. It is speculation, and the discussion presented here suggests it is error." They continue in the same equivocal tone: "If a family, weighing all the factors affecting their own circumstances, decides to use this modality, we are confident that they are not using an abortifacient."[53]

Of course, clarifying inconvenient biological truths is beside the point. Don't be misled. This fracas is not caused by a simple scientific misunderstanding. If it were, pro-lifers would rush to support birth control methods that don't, as they say, "cause abortions," like the diaphragm, condom, cervical cap, and spermicides. But the pro-life forces aren't on record anywhere in favor of methods that keep sperm and egg apart. It appears impossible to find a single instance in which a pro-life group has anything good to say about any birth control method except natural family planning—a technique most notable for its high failure rate. Even the lowly condom, as we'll see later, disturbs them.

In fact, when they aren't claiming that birth control is abortion, their next big idea is that birth control is unsafe. As Dr. David Grimes, one of the world's leading experts on contraception, puts it, "Some anti-abortion groups describe a subtle blend of fake claims and real, but exaggerated, risks to frighten women." And as Grimes, and every other impartial observer, hastens to point out, "Ironically, the net effect of this campaign to discredit contraception is more unplanned pregnancies and, of course, more abortions."[54] A classic example is the Web site for Physicians for Life that lists not one positive item about birth control in its numerous sections devoted to the subject. Instead, its headlines read: "The Pill Puts Women at Much Higher Risk of HIV and Other STDs," "Gel to Stop STDs

Holds Empty Promise," "Negative Effects of Vasectomy," "New Research Shows Dangers of Condoms in HIV Prevention," and "Oral Contraceptives May Reduce Sense of Smell."[55] The American Life League distributes scare pamphlets on every form of birth control. They are designed to look and read just like the ones you'd find in your doctor's office. Each explains why you shouldn't use a birth control method. One titled *Answers to Your Questions about Condoms and Spermicides* lists only the potential and rare negative side effects of both methods and offers no description of the benefits of either. The pamphlet ends with this message: "Condoms and spermicides fail to prevent the conception of babies, and they are potentially harmful! Be good to yourself. Don't use condoms and spermicides." The only three sources cited in the endnotes section of the pamphlet are a pro-life book opposing every birth control method, an outspoken pro-life physician, and a condom fact sheet produced by the American Life League itself.[56]

If a pro-life group does promote a form of family planning, it is always natural family planning. Terrifically unpopular as a contraceptive method (less than 2 percent of American women attempt it),[57] it is also extraordinarily unreliable, with a typical failure rate of 25 percent. (Of course, some pro-life groups even oppose natural family planning because they believe it is immoral for sexually active people to use any method to prevent pregnancy.) But for most mainstream pro-life groups it is the only birth control technique they promote. Yet the theory behind natural family planning, it turns out, is also based on a false understanding of science and the human reproductive system. Pro-life groups allege that a woman can be taught to recognize when she is ovulating and, therefore, can prevent pregnancy by avoiding having sex during that time. But new research raises doubts over whether it is possible to reliably know when a woman is ovulating. A study published in the journal *Fertility and Sterility* and funded by the Canadian Institutes of Health Research found that as many as 40 percent of women may develop "preovulatory follicles" two or three times during their menstrual cycle.[58] If the appropriate signals are received, these women have the biological potential to ovulate at different times during the cycle, not just once, as formerly thought. The premise behind natural family planning is that a woman ovulates at a predictable time, and only once, during her cycle. The current research is questioning this assumption. What we are now learning is that natural family planning may not only be difficult to practice, it just might be impossible altogether. The senior author of the study explained, "We all know people trying to use natural family planning, and we have a word for those people. We call them parents."[59]

Though many pro-life groups like to disguise their anti–birth control agendas, one pro-life group proudly proclaims it. The American Life League declares itself "the nation's largest pro-life educational organization with more than 300,000 supporters."[60] A.L.L.'s president, Judie Brown, was introduced in the book *The Right-to-Lifers* this way: "If any single person is responsible for the growth of the right-to-life movement, that person is Judie Brown."[61] And with a budget of more than $7 million, A.L.L. can bankroll just about any campaign it pleases.[62] A.L.L. is a prolific producer of anti–birth control materials, some evidence of which can be found in the 140 chapters of its *Pro-Life Activist's Encyclopedia.*[63] Chapter 104, "Artificial Contraception: Contrary to God's Plan," explains what seems like the true justification for all of its efforts:

God would not allow a baby to be conceived unless He had a purpose for that baby. Therefore, if we use contraception, we are denying God His purpose and we are saying "NO!" to His plan. . . . As a
species, we seem to have lost sight of our role and purpose on this
earth. God created the universe and everything in it for His pleasure not ours! He created us to give Him glory, not just recreate the
world and its natural laws to make our lives easier and more pleas-
urable.[64]

A.L.L. is unapologetically against every single form of birth control. It, of course, claims the most commonly used forms cause
abortions and defines its legislative goal to include "a legal ban on
abortifacient birth control."[65] They conducted a campaign against
contraceptive-coverage benefits for federal employees. In this effort, Judie Brown, A.L.L. president, explained, "We have been
working for over a year to prove that prescription contraceptives
have nothing to do with a woman's health and well-being but are
recreational drugs that prevent fertilization and abort children."[66]
She elaborates: "Depo-Provera, Norplant, the IUD and the pill can
kill tiny boys and girls and it is imperative that the government get
out of the deadly birth control business and take action to protect
all innocent human beings equally—without discrimination."[67] In
1996, A.L.L. picketed Searle Pharmaceutical Company just because it manufactures the standard birth control pill.[68]

What becomes clear from any examination of right-to-life groups
like A.L.L.—and keep in mind that A.L.L. not only is well funded
but also claims a large following and a record of success—is that, for
them, *trying to prevent a pregnancy is indistinguishable from trying
to end one.* Indeed, and this is why science matters so little to them,

they believe somehow that avoiding abortion is the first step in having an abortion. As the *Pro-Life Activist's Encyclopedia* explains:

> Contraception cannot be separated from abortion. In fact, anyone
> who debates on the topic of abortion will inevitably be drawn to the
> topic of artificial contraception over and over again, especially in
> the post-*Roe* era of pro-life activism. Therefore, every pro-life ac-
> tivist should understand the many relationships between abortion
> and artificial contraception. How does contraception lead to abor-
> tion? Quite simply, they are *virtually indistinguishable* in a psycho-
> logical, physical, and legal sense. . . . Those individuals who use
> artificial contraception take the critical step of separating sex from
> procreation. Contraception *not abortion* was the first step down the
> slippery slope.[69]

If they really wanted to stop abortion, the path to that goal is
fairly clear. Countries with the lowest rates of abortion are characterized, interestingly, by liberal abortion laws, well-financed contraception programs, and a commitment to comprehensive sex
education that includes teaching children about contraception.
These countries also differ from the United States in that they do
not have a powerful pro-life movement fighting efforts that clearly
reduce the need for abortion. But National Right to Life won't be
sending research staffers over to Sweden or the Netherlands—two
countries with the lowest abortion rates—anytime soon.

The reason, clearly, is that reducing the need for abortion is simply not the point. Keeping birth control from Americans, strangely,
is—and, beyond that, so is redefining how Americans think about
sex. Underpinning the pro-life movement's emotion about abortion

and contraception is an unyielding view of sex, its purpose and its pleasures. The never-shy Mrs. Brown is eager to explain, "Healthy women do not need to be immunized from their own children. Rather, men and women who participate in sexual intercourse need to know that children are an intended purpose of intercourse, and parents should therefore act to responsibly care for and protect their pre-born children."[70] Pro-life groups are not merely anti-abortion and anti–birth control. They are against sex and the sex lives the vast majority of Americans enjoy.

chapter two

Love (and Life) American Style

LET'S CONSIDER FOR A MOMENT that odd duck, the average American, more surveyed and studied, charted and graphed than probably any bird in history—nothing has been left out of the investigation of who we are and what we do, especially not our sex lives. A sweeping 2004 poll by ABC News/*PrimeTime Live,* one of the largest, most detailed looks at our sexual habits, revealed that the average American has sex once a week, and that's any adult, married or single. It doesn't matter if you're conservative or liberal, devout or atheist. If you're in a relationship, then 85 percent of you have sex every week.[1]

This is a bulldozer of a statistic. Let's reflect on it for a moment. It speaks volumes about how we live and love. You don't have to be a fan of *Sex and the City* to understand that sex is one activity we are all committed to. And it's not just something we do; it's really part of who we are. Discussions about who should have sex and why are largely decorative (or, perhaps, just titillating). Sexual liberation is passé. Women *are* sexually liberated, right-wing, churchgoing women too.

To understand the competing agendas of the pro-choice and pro-life movements, it's essential to consider the central role of sex in our lives. After all, the debate about abortion, like the debate about birth control, is rooted in an argument about sex. Specifically, it's an argument about why people have sex, or why they *should* have sex. The pro-lifers want sex to be a means to an end. That end is a baby. "If you are using any kind of birth control—stop," says Randall Terry, founder of Operation Rescue. "Leave the number of children you have in God's hands."[2] This wish necessarily colors their thinking about contraception, as well as abortion. (You can't think the sole purpose of sex is to make a baby and also be for birth control.)

Sex-as-baby-making-tool may be what pro-lifers long for, but it clearly doesn't correspond to how we live (not if you're going to enjoy sex once a week). Sex is, and pro-choicers embrace this fact, a recreational activity too. It's not bowling. It comes from intimacy and also produces intimacy. But people do it for the pleasure it brings, and not just for the baby it might produce. Pro-choicers view contraception as an essential support for this lifestyle; the control it offers is, for the pro-choice side, a positive. Think about it. What would life be like for that average American polled by ABC if they didn't have birth control? The typical American woman, the one having sex every week, would be pregnant year in and year out. Bear in mind that the average woman is fertile for nearly thirty years of her life (fifteen to forty-five are the reproductive ages). She devotes approximately seven of those years either attempting to become pregnant, actually being pregnant, or breast-feeding—and when breast-feeding the chance of pregnancy is greatly diminished. But for the remaining twenty-three years, on average, she's trying not to have kids.

Pro-lifers, in a pinch, may recognize this as reality, but they find it lamentable. (In this debate they are the moralists, the scolders.) To be pro-life means more than taking a stand against abortion. Abortion is that movement's rhetorical leading edge—*baby killer* is an attention-getting sound bite—but in the pro-life scheme of things, it is just one issue, and not the guiding one. Pro-lifers would like to change our views on sex (and on the roles of women as well—more on that later). Read widely in pro-life writings and you'll come away convinced that women who use birth control (the pro-life establishment calls us "contraceptors") in order to enjoy weekly sex are indulgent and selfish. "Most people in the pro-life movement have a certain morality and believe sex is not for fun and games," says Joseph Scheidler, founder of the Pro-Life Action League. "I think contraception is disgusting, people using each other for pleasure."[3]

The pro-choice movement is comfortable with sex and contraception. Perhaps it is simply a prejudice in favor of the practical. (If pro-lifers are the moralists, the pro-choicers are the pragmatists.) Pro-lifers want to change the way we live; pro-choicers want to help us lead the lives we choose, without dangerous consequences. The pro-lifer may find our appetite for sex "disgusting," but the pro-choice person accepts how we are, and celebrates it. Sex isn't an evil if not done with procreation in mind. Just the opposite. For the person living in a pro-choice world, sex makes us happier, healthier, and, perhaps, even better parents.

Consider a groundbreaking 2004 study published in the esteemed journal *Science*. The researchers, one a Nobel Prize winner, assessed how more than nine hundred women spent their time and how much satisfaction they experienced in various activities. The researchers attempted to discover how women and men pursue happiness. Participants systematically reconstructed their activities. And the activity that made women happiest was sex; it brings them more happiness than eating, socializing, and relaxing.[4] Another study conducted by two economists found that regular sex brings people as much happiness as a $50,000-a-year raise. "The more sex," they researchers write, "the happier the person."[5] As weird as it sounds, our sex lives turn out to be more important than our work lives or even our health status as a predictor of happiness.

There's a good chance we're biologically built for solely-for-pleasure sex. Evolution (or possibly the intelligent designer) may have engineered us that way. In 2004, *Time* featured a cover story on the health benefits of sex and reported, "Studies are showing that arousal and an active sex life may lead to a longer life, better heart health, an improved ability to ward off pain, a more robust immune system and even protection against certain cancers, not to mention lower rates of depression."[6]

Some experts believe that our appetite for recreational sex may make us better parents, too, more able to care for our babies for as long as we do. Human children are unusual in that they are dependent on their parents for much longer than the offspring of other animals. Also, human adult females are different from adult females of most other species in that our fertile periods are hidden, unknown to potential sex partners or even to women themselves. (Females of most species let suitors know when they're fertile with obvious signs, like shiny red butts.) The lengthy dependence of our children and the mysteriousness of our fertile times are, biologists believe, connected.

In the animal kingdom, most females are single moms; males are useful as impregnators and then should be on their way. Luckily, most newborn mammals help themselves to food as soon as they're weaned. With human kids, it's years before they feed themselves. Pulitzer Prize–winning author and physiologist Jared Diamond explains how our foremothers solved this problem in his book *Why Is Sex Fun? The Evolution of Human Sexuality*.

Her brilliant solution: remain sexually receptive even after ovulating! Keep him satisfied by copulating whenever he wants! In that way, he'll hang around, have no need to look for new sex partners, and will even share his daily hunting bag of meat. Recreational sex is thus supposed to function as the glue holding a human couple together while they cooperate in rearing their helpless baby. That in essence is the theory . . . and it seems to have much to recommend it.[7]

In this context, birth control, and the type of sex it permits, shouldn't be seen as disgusting. It may even allow for the fulfillment of a woman's biological destiny; she can have sex, improve her health, tend her relationship, and not be overrun with children she cannot care for.

As any casual observer knows, it's this happy, eager view of sex that is reflected everywhere in today's culture. (Like it or not, we live in a pro-choice world.) Sex pervades popular culture. It's used banally to move products, from shampoo to cars. It's a part of our pop culture experience. TV characters lead full sex lives in plain view—even Homer and Marge have an occasional romp in the hay. The big worry over sex is not when or if—but excellence. To take the 2005 newsstands as one indicator, you'd think that Americans were angling to perfect sex through daily practice. Sex, in these mass-market magazines, is hardly a utilitarian exercise designed to efficiently produce a bouncing baby. It's a culture of secrets that need to be unlocked, and then enjoyed, just for themselves. *Self* magazine's cover proclaimed, "Make sex better every day! Boost your know how, your satisfaction."[8] *Men's Health* prescribed "30 sizzling sex secrets" to "unleash in bed" (not the next time you are trying to impregnate your wife but rather) "tonight."[9] We are, it's easy to conclude, sex-obsessed. Still, that doesn't mean we're destined to be vixens or sexual predators or lifestyle experimenters.

In fact, the vast majority of us are monogamous; most prefer marriage. Unmarried couples living together today, a now common arrangement, are as monogamous as married couples.[10] Indeed, despite what the apocalyptic rhetoric suggests, the past century has actually witnessed a steep decline in extramarital affairs. Studies conducted by the famous sex researcher Alfred Kinsey, both in 1948 and 1953, found that 26 percent of women and a whopping 50 percent of men had had an extramarital sexual experience. Similar findings were discovered by earlier studies conducted by researchers in the 1920s. But today in our sex-saturated culture the number of married people who have had an extramarital affair has plummeted, according to one authoritative source, to 6 percent of women and 10 percent of men.[11] (Other more conservative sources estimate the rate of extramarital affairs today somewhat higher, but still half the 1950s rate.)[12]

The upturn in fidelity seems a clear result of many of those things that drive pro-lifers wild: the more lengthy and thoughtful trying-out of marriage partners, the freer expression within marriage of different desires. Most important, perhaps, is that today society accepts our sexual urges. Sexual desire isn't marginalized, isn't correct in some instances and disgusting in others. It just is. This may be contrary to what the pro-life movement wants (some pro-life thinkers even condemn masturbation).* But like it or not, we live in a pro-choice culture. Not only is sex-for-pleasure an ex-

---

*Prolife.com's home page asks, "What about Masturbation?" If a visitor clicks on the hyperlinked question, they learn: "Masturbation is a homosexual act: sex with a person of the same sex, namely yourself."

pected part of life, but birth control is one of the foundations on which we build our lives.

In one thing, pro-lifers are right. When they target family planning, they take aim at something important. Birth control has led to a transformation of our society, one so sweeping and rapid that only recently have we had the occasion to take stock of its impact. The pro-choice movement, which grew out of the contraception movement, has long understood that these were the stakes. It's no coincidence that Margaret Sanger, founder of Planned Parenthood and mother of the American birth control movement, and Marie Stopes, her European counterpart, wrote books on how this technology would change society. As they envisioned it, the first change would be in marriages.[13] They knew that family planning is essential to a more perfect union between husband and wife. They also knew that sex was to be enjoyed. (Sanger was an early sexologist, the Dr. Ruth of her time, whose book scandalously gave explicit instructions on better sex.) The movements they founded fought against pernicious, puritan views on sex; they understood that a society in which sex for pleasure was an accepted part of the human condition could change the world—that is, if birth control were legal, which was not the case in Sanger's time. Margaret Sanger, as Ellen Chesler put it in her seminal biography of the leader, understood that contraception "would be a tool for redistributing power fundamentally, in the bedroom, the home, and the larger community."[14]

Sanger and her colleagues were not suggesting anything that the most comfortable in society didn't already practice; at the turn of the century, the wealthy already had private contraceptive arrangements. Physicians conspired with their well-heeled patients in what was then a criminal act. In the 1920s, an exhaustive scientific study of the sex life of 1,000 well-educated married women revealed that a full 74 percent used contraceptive methods themselves and gave their approval to them. Economic and health reasons and the desire for a satisfactory married life were cited as equally important motives.[15] Another survey, conducted in 1929, of 2,200 women revealed widespread support for honest approaches to people's real sex lives. It found that 84 percent of women believed married couples were justified in having intercourse not for the purpose of having children; 63 percent thought information on birth control should be available to unmarried people (and even 72 percent felt that there were acceptable reasons for abortion to be performed).[16]

Despite its widespread use, at least among the affluent, it wasn't until 1965 that the Supreme Court ruled that birth control was legal for married couples. The Court didn't grant unmarried people legal access to birth control until 1972 (a year before abortion was legalized). For many in the pro-life movement, these dates mark the period in which everything started to go wrong: from the breakdown of the nuclear family to a generalized increase in permissiveness and a denigration of American morals. For many pro-life conservatives, it's the period before birth control was legalized that serves as a kind of sentimental attachment, and also a model. It's the fifties wife and mother who seemed to have it together. Even today, June Cleaver is the benchmark mom to whom every other mother is compared. What was the reality for the pre–birth control mom, though?

In her masterful book *The Way We Never Were: American Families and the Nostalgia Trap,* historian Stephanie Coontz explains that in the fifties, birth rates soared, doubling the time devoted to child care.[17] Consequently, women's educational parity with men dropped sharply, while their housework time increased exponentially—despite having new "time-saving" household technologies.[18] And with women assigned to endless tasks in the home, men shouldered the full responsibility of supporting the family economically. One dire consequence was that one in four Americans in the mid-1950s lived in poverty.[19] By the end of the 1950s, one-third of American children lived in poverty. Even among white families in the fifties, one-third could not get by on the income of the household head.[20]

As Coontz explains, in the days before birth control the role of mother was forced on many women. Women's rights were limited, but social pressure could be even more daunting. Coontz cites a study of hospitalized "schizophrenic" women in the San Francisco Bay area during the 1950s. "Institutionalization and sometimes electric shock treatments were used to force women to accept their domestic roles and their husband's dictates," she concludes. "Shock treatments also were recommended for women who sought abortion, on the assumption that failure to want a baby signified dangerous emotional disturbance."[21] Let's not forget that in this golden age of motherhood, women were deeply mistrusted. They were, as Coontz points out, often denied the right to serve on juries, sign contracts, or take out credit cards in their own name.[22] A 1954 article in *Esquire* called working wives a "menace"; a *Life* author termed married women's employment a "disease." In some states, the law gave husbands total control over family finances. "There were," as Coontz continues, "not many permissible alternatives to baking brownies, experimenting with new canned soups, and getting rid of stains around the collar."[23] Not surprisingly, national polls conducted during the fifties found that 20 percent of all couples considered their marriages unhappy.[24] Researchers in the fifties found in surveys of working-class couples that slightly less than one-third reported being happily or very happily married.[25]

Part of the reason for unhappiness in fifties marriages was that many couples didn't really want to be married in the first place. They were trapped into marriage by unintended pregnancy. With no sex ed, no birth control, no legal abortion—the exact legislative agenda of today's pro-life movement!—teen birth rates soared, reaching highs that have not been equaled since.

Once birth control became legal nationwide, and especially after the introduction of the instantly popular birth control pill, women's lives were transformed. June Cleaver became Hillary Clinton. The change was almost instantaneous, and most people understood the cause. In 1999, a Gallup poll revealed that more people cited birth control as having the "highest impact" on women than "opportunity for higher education," "access to jobs," "political representation," or even the much-publicized "women's movement."[26]

Given the option, more and more women decided to postpone marriage and parenthood. In 1970 the average age of a new mother was twenty-one; by 2000, the average age of a woman at first birth was twenty-eight.[27] "The pill enabled young men and women to put off marriage while not having to put off sex," report Harvard researchers Claudia Goldin and Lawrence Katz in their 2002 study, "The Power of the Pill," published in the *Journal of Political Economy*. "Sex no longer had to be packaged with commitment devices, many of which encouraged early marriage."

The Pill didn't just alter marriage, which was no longer a gateway to sex. In the span of just four decades, we have witnessed a massive transformation of society. Women rushed into college so quickly, so enthusiastically, that today the concern is more likely to be about men's equity—women now represent 61 percent of undergraduates. From 1970 to 2000, the number of women graduating college more than doubled.[28] Women are currently in the majority of those in medical school and seeking postgraduate degrees, and they equal the number of men in law school.[29]

The surge of women entering college and the professions seemed to happen almost immediately after the legalization of contraception. Goldin and Katz, who studied the effects of the Pill, found that "the percentage of all lawyers and judges who are women more than doubled in the 1970s (from 5.1 percent in 1970 to 13.6 percent in 1980) and was 29.7 percent in 2000. The share of female physicians increased from 9.1 percent in 1970 to 14.1 in 1980 and was 27.9 percent in 2000. Similar patterns hold for occupations such as dentists, architects, veterinarians, economists, and most of the engineering fields."[30]

Given the opportunity to delay marriage and childbearing, women entered the workforce and never left. Whereas in 1943 the majority of women stated that they preferred not to hold a job, by 1979 only a stunning 5 percent of women held this view.[31] In just two decades after the legalization of family planning, the number of women in the workforce nearly doubled. (In 1965, 25 million women were in the workforce. By 1984, 46 million were—slightly more than half of all American women at the time.)[32] Today, there are nearly equal numbers of women as men in the workforce.[33]

The ramifications of women's entry into the workplace are well known—and for the most part beneficial. Indeed, those frightening fifties statistics indicating widespread poverty and marital unhappiness have improved. The rate of poverty today is half what it was in the 1950s;[34] the percentage of children living in poverty has decreased 50 percent since 1959.[35] More than twice as many married Americans today report being "very happy" in their marriage.[36] And the rate of teen motherhood has been reduced by more than half.[37]

This new pro-choice society of the past three or four decades has given all women, regardless of their political views, more options (and as we'll see, men's options have expanded too). This includes even those women who choose full-time motherhood. Staying at home to raise children remains an opportunity, and now a more flexible and inviting one because the option to segue back into the workforce exists.

Even though many sentimentally regard a stay-at-home mother as the choice of greater virtue, most women don't. The vast majority of working mothers believe that employment has no impact on the quality of their relationship with their kids.[38] Astonishing as it seems, most working women today say they would continue working even if they had the option of staying home.[39] One study found that one in two of the very homemakers the pro-lifers see as leading the most laudable life would, given the chance to start over, choose to have a career. By contrast, only one in five working mothers said she'd like to leave her job to stay home with her children.[40] For many women, working outside the home *is* their family value. By providing more economic support for the family, workforce moms view their careers not only as a way to fulfill something in themselves but also as a chance to secure more options for their children.

Yet so much has been written about the horrors working women have unleashed on their children. It's a virtual cottage industry of the religious pro-life Right, which has originated many of the attacks. "Latch-key kids," a favorite phrase in the 1980s, helped cement in the public's mind the unsupported notion that mothers at work meant neglect of their kids. In the mid-eighties, conservative, pro-life activist Phyllis Schafly suggested that mothers who remained employed for their own "self-fulfillment" had contributed to adolescent suicides.[41] The anti–working-woman climate of the eighties included constant media coverage of what was made to seem like widespread satanic, ritualistic sex abuse in day-care centers. Between 1977 and 1985, the number of children in day care nearly quadrupled as women rushed into the workplace.[42] No doubt, some mothers felt guilty about turning their kids over to strangers. Now, suddenly the airwaves were saturated with stories of horrific satanic cults in day-care centers. A search of newspaper articles in the 1980s found that stories about alleged cases of child abuse, child "satanism," and sexual predators rose from a few dozen a year to more than four hundred a year.[43] Many of the cases that dominated the national discourse in the eighties never led to convictions. Of the thirty cases that went to trial, more than half the judgments of juries and prosecutors would later be overturned by appellate judges. A decade later, sociologists wondered how so many spurious cases could come about at once.[44] "It seems it had something to do about this fear that we'd turned our kids over to total strangers," says Catherine Beckett, a University of Michigan sociologist. "It's as if there was a guilt that people we didn't know were raising them for us."[45]

There may indeed have been some abuse as the child-care industry grew rapidly to meet the demands brought about by the new norm of two parents in the workforce. But in the eighties when this hysteria hit, a child was considerably more likely to be sexually abused by a priest or a family member than a child-care worker. This frenzy seemed fed by a cultural backlash aimed at mothers heartless enough to send their children to day care.

Ever since they first donned those shoulder-padded suits, working women have been blamed for many of societal ills. Poor test scores, attention deficit disorder, school shootings, sexually active teens, or secret torture chambers under day-care centers have all been served up as evidence that society is paying dearly for mothers seeking "selfish gratification" through careers rather than exclusively tending to hearth and home.

Pro-life groups have continually sounded the theme, encouraging women (never men) to abandon their careers for the sake of their children. In the early nineties, the likes of then-representative William Dannemeyer, a pro-life Republican from California, took to the floor of the House of Representatives to denounce the "devastation" that results when working mothers "put careers ahead of children and rationalize material benefits in the name of children."[46] More recently, pro-life radio bully Laura Schlessinger authored the vindictively anti-working-mother book subtitled *Don't Have Them If You Won't Raise Them.* In Schlessinger's view, "career" is pitted against "family" as if the two could never be compatible. In 2005, a "fellow" at Concerned Women for America continued the battering of the "selfish" working mother, writing, "Nature will not forever be denied; women are beginning to see the costs of imbibing the unnatural cocktail of self-centeredness served up by me-centered post-modernism. . . . For many women, the career track that lured so enticingly has become a daily grind that merely pays the bills; a treadmill that is no golden pathway to their dreams."[47] (It is interesting that the pro-life critique is inevitably aimed at some middle- or upper-middle-class mom who supposedly has the choice not to work. In the pro-life view, most women work not because they have bills to pay but because of some self-indulgent whim.)

The pro-life camp offers an unending monologue about how "pro-child" they are. Yet in a kind of twisted logic, pro-life operatives have sought to "defend" children by trying to make it harder to be a working parent. For example, most of the Senate opposition to the Family Medical Leave Act was from pro-lifers.[48] A law much cherished by the American people, the Family Medical Leave Act allows working parents, for the first time in U.S. history, to take leave from work to care for a newborn. Wouldn't this be *exactly* the type of legislation that makes it easier to have a baby and raise a happy one? Ninety percent of the senators who voted against the Family Medical Leave Act are fervently pro-life.[49]

Unfortunately, this is typical behavior for the supposedly "pro-child" pro-lifers. The Children's Defense Fund, the premiere national children's advocacy group (an organization that takes no position in the abortion debate), recently released its 2004 congressional rankings of the best and worst legislators for children. The organization used twelve indicators to rank senators and members of Congress, counting their votes on issues ranging from safety locks on guns to education spending. It should be a sobering shock that of the 113 representatives the Children's Defense Fund classifies as the *worst* for children, 100 percent are pro-life.[50] The pro-life movement mobilized countless volunteers and invested stunningly large sums to elect those who actively work to strip children of basic protections—educational funding, health care, unemployment benefits for their parents—the very things that make it easier for a family to have, and raise, a child. And those ranked as *best* legislators for children? Ninety-five percent are pro-choice.[51]

In her book *Is the Fetus a Person? A Comparison of Policies across the Fifty States,* Jean Reith Schroedel compares pro-life and pro-choice states in how they treat children.[52] She found that

> no evidence was found that pro-life states have adopted a comprehensive range of policies designed to protect and assist the weakest and most vulnerable in our society. Instead, the opposite appeared to be true. . . . Pro-choice states were more likely to favor adoption and to provide aid to needy children. Simply, pro-life states make it difficult for women to have abortions, but they do not help these women provide for the children once born. Pro-life states also spend less money per pupil on kindergarten through twelfth grade education."[53]

Schroedel concludes, "Pro-choice states are more committed to providing for the society's weakest and most vulnerable than are pro-life states."[54]

It is a sad irony that the sharpest attacks not only on working women but also on child care are part of the broad agenda of many national pro-life groups, like Focus on the Family, the Family Research Council, and Concerned Women for America. Concerned Women for America was founded by Tim LaHaye and his wife, Beverly. Tim LaHaye is better know as the author of the "Left Behind" series, which details the events surrounding the Christian Right's much anticipated "rapture." In his nonfiction work, LaHaye has sketched a religious-Right utopia where there is no separation of church and state. Abortion is outlawed, and women, in

LaHaye's vision, "stay home to raise their babies," renounce feminism, and obey their husbands as "the spiritual head of the family."[55] In keeping with this vision, Concerned Women for America leads campaigns against contraception and the earliest abortion methods. Its Web site includes articles such as "Career or Family?" (an important enough question that it was assigned to two, one should assume childless, interns; the interns' answer: stay home). At Concerned Women for America, at least, there's no hypocrisy. Working women there lead the life they preach. Indeed, even if it sounds rather quaint to the rest of us, this organization enforces the mothers-should-be-mothers-only lifestyle. In 1997, the *Washington Post* described conditions this way, "When working women become pregnant at Concerned Women for America, a conservative advocacy group in Washington, their boss tells them, 'Congratulations! You've just gotten a promotion in life: being a full-time mom.' There is no paid maternity leave, and almost all new mothers there quit to stay home full time."[56]

Certainly, the attack on child care has evolved. No longer is the child-care worker the monster. Now it's the experience of spending time away from mom that damages kids. It's as if the very idea of professional child care is corrupting, harmful. And how nicely this serves the pro-life agenda. For example, the Illinois Right to Life Committee reports on its Web site, "Study finds day care detrimental to children."[57] Lifesite, an international pro-life Web site, helped promote fears of child care with an article titled "World's Foremost Child Care Study Shows Day Care Leads to Aggression." The pro-life Family Research Council hosted a forum about the book *Day Care Deception: What the Child Care Establishment Isn't Telling Us.* The book was written by Brian Robertson, a fellow at the pro-life

Howard Center for Family, Religion, and Society—an organization with a mission to "affirm that the natural human family is established by the Creator" and that the ideas that followed the introduction of the Pill "challenge the family's very legitimacy as an institution." Needless to say, Robertson believes that child care is a feminist plot. "The new feminist version of women's empowerment requires all mothers to pursue careers and be economically independent of their husbands," explains Robertson, adding, "It cannot abide the realities of motherhood."[58]

All the protest against day care, remember, stems from a deep distrust of independent working women, who in turn have flourished as the result of birth control. Yet it turns out that the facts about child care, when viewed without a political agenda, tell a more positive story. The allegations that day care is detrimental to children are at best exaggerated, at worst outright lies. Most of the recent attacks are based on one study, which continues to be debated even among the twenty-nine researchers who authored it. Jay Belsky, a professor at the University of London, is the only researcher of the bunch to claim that nonmaternal care can lead to more aggressive behaviors in some children. For the record, Belsky is not against child care and even helped found an infant day-care center as a professor at Pennsylvania State University in the seventies.[59] Belsky's contention, and the source of all this controversy, is that 17 percent of kids in day care show more aggressive behaviors than those in maternal care. And, by the way, that "acting out" behavior disappears by age three.[60] Still, Belsky tends to find the fraction that misbehave through age two significant, much more than any of his colleagues. (As one puts it, "We're not seeing that child care produces super-aggressive kids.")[61] But the important point is what does his finding *mean*? Is it, as the pro-life side asserts, a condemnation of any woman who would risk her child in day care? Or is it a call for improved quality of child care? Belsky himself isn't sure. "It could have led to the conclusion that we should have more parental leave; it might have drawn the conclusion that we should assure that our care is of the highest quality," Belsky explained in an interview.[62]

All of this creates an alarming pattern. First, pro-life groups work to keep birth control from women; concurrently, they assert that child care is bad, an assertion that carries with it the implication that women who rely on child care are bad as well. These accusations, these complaints, come with no accompanying solution—except that women should stay at home, caring for their young. The pro-life movement has no campaign under way to devote *more* funding to make quality child care more available or affordable, or better.

Despite the punitive rhetoric on the Right (bolstered, as always, by a nostalgia for a way they imagine the world once was), the truth is that women flooded into the workplace *not* because they are uniquely selfish creatures who don't care about their children. Working women themselves tell a different story. They believe that a happy mom is a better mom. Don't forget those surveys that show that half of today's stay-at-home moms would, if they had another chance, pursue a career. Or that only 20 percent of women in the workforce would rather be that idealized stay-at-homer. Not only that, but many also believe that having more balance in their lives—being both a breadwinner and a PTA member—makes them better mothers.

But happiness or contentedness—or, as the conservatives disparagingly call it, "self-fulfillment"—is hardly the only benefit of

women. (And, by the way, women are more likely to be happy with their jobs than men.)[63] The misguided assumption here is that most women *choose* to go to work. But for most mothers, of course, working is an economic necessity, and one that has led to important benefits: they've made their families wealthier. This is, perhaps, the greatest single remedy to poverty since the New Deal. Earnings of working wives markedly lower the incidence of poverty for all ethnic and racial groups. Families in which husbands and wives both work are much less likely to experience poverty than families in which only husbands work. In fact, families in which the husband is the sole breadwinner are four times more likely to be poor than those in which the wife brings home an income.[64] When both partners work, they earn incomes nearly two-thirds more than those of families in which the husband alone works.[65] Money may not be everything. But it's something.

Women's equality and careers have created higher incomes, and higher incomes lead to lower divorce rates. Financial stress is one of the most common reasons cited by divorced couples. Just 5 percent of those living in households with an income of $50,000 or more say they are currently separated or divorced. At the other extreme, 38 percent of those who live in households with less than $20,000 in income say they are separated or divorced.[66]

So what of the effects on children? Between 1980 and 2000, the percentage of children living in dual-income families doubled.[67] As the twenty-nine researchers of the much-debated study on the effects of child care explain, whatever role child care plays, family income plays a much more important role in child development. In fact, it's more significant than most anything else, including whether a child spends the day with mom or in a day-care environment. In a family where the mother has a higher education (more true of working women), where there is less financial stress (as in dual-earning homes), children do better developmentally, the studies find. "Countless studies have shown that family income is associated with children's development and educational attainment," adds W. Jean Yeung, lead author of a study on how income affects preschoolers' cognitive abilities and behavior. The first item on a list of things "to improve low-income, young children's cognitive achievement," says Yeung, is "to offer programs that seek to raise income levels." By the same token, if behavioral problems are the issue, then, says Yeung, "we should focus on strategies to reduce income instability."[68] It's not time with children that seems to be the issue—those endless, lazy days that pro-lifers dream of—but what mothers do with that time that counts. And it turns out that the woman who has benefited from the pro-choice revolution, the educated mom, is the mom more likely to read to her children every day and provide more cognitively stimulating play. Seventy-three percent of children whose mothers are college educated were read to every day, compared to 49 percent of children whose mother had only a high school education.[69]

Perhaps what is most surprising, and fascinating, about all this is that working mothers today are not only spending different- (and better-) quality time with their kids but actually spending *more* time than did the stay-at-home mothers of the past. The work-family balance we've been striving for over the past three decades appears to be taking shape.

The Institute for Social Research at the University of Michigan did a lengthy and comprehensive study of the time families spend together over nearly two decades. The study, called *Changes in*

Children's Time with Parents, U.S., 1981–1997,[70] had some startling findings. In 1981, children three to twelve years old averaged
twenty-five hours a week with their moms and nineteen hours with
their dads. But by 1997, at a time when women were entering the
workforce like never before, kids averaged thirty-one hours a week
with their moms and twenty-three hours with their dads. And this
wasn't the parents reporting time spent (and possibly overreporting out of guilt): it's the kids' version. Although this study did find
that today's stay-at-home moms spend more time with their children than do working mothers, another found that the first generation of men raised by working mothers (men now in their thirties
and younger) are significantly more likely than previous generations to feel that a mother who works outside the home can have
just as good a relationship with her children as a mother who is not
employed.[71] It's not just the number of hours. Clearly, today's
working women, perhaps because they do work, put a greater value
on spending time with their children.

Another stunning finding is how much *men* have changed as a result of women's equality. This message is lost on pro-lifers. The dynamic of the family has changed. Men have more freedom,
flexibility, and choices now too. The University of Michigan study
found that children's time with their fathers increased significantly
only in families in which the mother worked outside the home.[72]
As researchers of the Families and Work Institute summed up,
"There are many other indications that the workforce has become
more family-friendly—especially the fact that American fathers are
spending more time with their children than fathers did a generation ago." This trait seems to be passed along in the DNA of a new
workforce. Gen-X fathers spend significantly more time with their

children than baby-boomer fathers—a difference of more than one hour each day. And most men are aware of this difference: 84 percent report that they spend more time with their kids than their fathers did.[73] As the researchers point out, "Obviously, this trend is affected by the increase in the number of employed mothers." Today, more husbands count on their wives to bring home a significant share of the family wealth; nearly one in four women now earns more than her husband.[74] With this, men have options to leave a negative work environment, change careers, take more career risks, and be more involved with their children.

Today, as a result of not having to shoulder *all* the economic demands of the family, and by having smaller families, men have been allowed to become more involved fathers—better fathers—than ever before. They seem to like being fathers in a way that is new and real. Eighty-five percent of dads say they get more joy out of fatherhood than their own fathers did.[75] Of course, you'd never know it if you listened to the so-called pro-family groups set on convincing us that the way we live now is tearing our country apart, family by family.

No doubt, some men are angered—silently or otherwise—by women in the workplace. The competition is keener than ever. Yet in the past thirty years, men have been transforming. Today, the majority of men say they desire an equal marriage (77 percent).[76] And they appear to mean it. Mothers spend thirty-six minutes less on chores on workdays, and one hour less on nonworkdays, than they did twenty-five years ago. Meanwhile, today men spend an hour more on chores on both work- and nonworkdays. Dads spend thirty minutes more each day helping their wives raise their children than they did twenty-five years ago.

Fathers' increased involvement starts at the very beginning of their children's lives: 90 percent of dads are present in the delivery room (compared to 10 percent in 1970).[77, 78] "Men are doing more changing, feeding and burping than they were 30 years ago," states James Levine, who heads the Manhattan-based Fatherhood Project at the Families and Work Institute. "At parent-teacher meetings," says Levine, "you're still going to see more women than men, but the number of men is increasing. We're seeing this across all income, racial, ethnic and geographic groups. It's a very broad-based social phenomenon."[79] Dads today are even more affectionate with their children: 60 percent hug their school-age kids every day, and 79 percent tell their children they love them several times a week.[80] "This is welcome news because it benefits the child," says Jaipaul L. Roopnarine, a professor of child studies at Syracuse University who has researched cross-cultural fathering for more than two decades. "Children whose fathers are involved with them show better education achievement, fewer problems in school, and they're better off socially."[81]

All this seems to have created a revolution in how men see themselves. Seventy percent of dads feel they would be just as effective staying home and raising children as their wives.[82] The Gallup organization found that one in four men would actually *like* to stay home and take care of the house and family.[83] Spike TV, the TV network for men, surveyed 1,300 men and found that the number considering staying home is even higher; the poll found that 56 percent of men would consider becoming stay-at-home dads. As the Spike TV pollsters explain, "This is the first generation of men to feel the full effect of women entering the workforce. As women have become partners in the workplace, men are now adjusting to a more equal status at home."[84] And record numbers of men are choosing to stay at home too. Today, statistics show that roughly 2.5 million dads nationwide stay at home to be their children's primary caretaker.

The unheralded result of women entering the workforce has been the rise of the real family man and the making of the more devoted father. It is to the point that the vast majority of men today, 72 percent, say they would sacrifice pay and job opportunities for more time with their families. Spike TV found that most men would choose attending their kids' sporting event over an important work obligation. The Spike TV pollsters explain, "There's been a paradigm shift. Men want involvement with kids. Even with infants, they get up at night. It was NEVER like this before. They're taking parenting seriously. New responsibilities with kids and in homes are enriching men's lives. They're excited by it, and proud."[85]

So much for the breakup of the family caused by women's emerging roles, the sexual revolution, and the birth control pill—family is more desired, and enjoyed, than ever before. With women sharing a larger stake in providing economically for the family, men have stepped up their investment in nurturing: indeed, today men in the United States are significantly more likely than women to think that "having a child is vital to their sense of self-fulfillment," according to one telling Gallup poll.[86]

Not only do we live in a culture largely produced by the prochoice movement, but we're lucky to do so. We accept that sex is sometimes only for pleasure and that birth control and family planning make this possible. This, of course, is contrary to what the pro-life movement wants for us. But the truth is that the fragile progress launched by the pro-choice movement has made women more content and their families happier and healthier.

chapter three

The Pro-Life Paradox

WHAT IF THE STRATEGIES of the pro-life movement have had the exact opposite effect of those they claim to desire? What if pro-life maneuvers have played an important role in encouraging abortions (including "partial birth abortions") and, at the same time, led to riskier sex—especially for teens?

For the most part, pro-lifers tend to be absolutists. For them, you are either churchgoer or sinner, procreator or contraceptor, for the culture of life or for the culture of death. Pro-choicers, by contrast, tend to be more pragmatic. There is always the life that we want to lead, whether we express it most fully on Sunday morning or, just as likely, Saturday night. And then, says the pro-choicer, comes Monday morning when you must weigh options and needs, and decide what's best for you and your family. For the pro-life movement, decision making is less complicated. For the unmarried, the right course is abstinence (which we'll discuss later). And for everyone, single or married, the right course never, ever leads to abortion. Unfortunately, if the goal is to reduce abortion, the pro-lifers' morally unambiguous strategies don't seem to work.

To begin with, criminalizing abortion may be a sacred pro-life goal. But in practice, bans have failed to curb rates of abortions.

Many countries that have outlawed abortion have *higher* abortion rates than countries where abortion is legal. Brazil, Chile, and Peru—in which the predominant religion is Catholicism—are among these.[1] (It's worth noting that the Church wasn't always pro-life. Until 1869, even the Catholic Church supported legalized abortion until quickening, at approximately nineteen weeks of pregnancy, which is when it considered the fetus was given a soul.)[2] The truth is that if abortion is outlawed, women don't seek services less frequently; they just survive them less often. This has been true in the United States (when abortion was illegal) as well as in many countries abroad today. In the late nineteenth century, when abortion was criminalized in the United States, an estimated 2 million abortions still occurred each year[3] (considerably more than take place today), and this was at a time when the U.S. population was one-fourth its current size.[4] One study estimated that in the 1920s, one in five pregnancies ended in illegal abortion, approximately the same as the abortion rate today.[5]

And it's not just pro-choice women who seek abortions, never has been. Most people would be startled to learn that even today, when battle lines are drawn, 40 percent of women who have abortions in the United States are Evangelical Christian or Catholic.[6] They are your average morality voter, your above-average churchgoer. In all likelihood, they call themselves pro-life. Even though the great wish of pro-lifers is to cast those seeking abortions as irresponsible daters, the actual statistics are more forgiving. The majority of women in the United States (61 percent) having abortions are already moms.[7]

Unable so far to criminalize abortions in the United States, the pro-life movement has taken up a strategy of incrementalism. It has strived to delay abortions, placing hurdle after hurdle in their way. The result has been, even by pro-life definitions, perverse. After all, the net effect hasn't been to stop abortions, but to postpone them until the fetus is more developed and the woman is at greater risk. This strategy is carried out even if it means forcing a woman to have one of those dreaded late-term abortions. Indeed, some of the later-term abortions—"partial-birth abortions," as the pro-life side labels them—no doubt occur as a result of campaigns waged by the pro-life movement.

Let's take a look at how this works. One favorite pro-life strategy is to pass laws that require a waiting period before a woman can obtain an abortion. Twenty-three states have enacted what are called "mandatory delay" laws; all are coupled with mandatory-counseling laws that typically require abortion clinics to dispense information designed to dissuade women from having an abortion.[8] Once a woman receives the counseling, she must wait, usually twenty-four hours, before she can obtain the abortion. The twenty-four-hour wait may seem inconsequential, but the effect on real lives is considerable. The series of small barriers often means scheduling two days of missed work or missed school, traveling long distances twice—don't forget, 87 percent of U.S. counties don't have an abortion provider—and even paying to stay overnight in a hotel.[9]

In fact, the statistics show that the mandatory delays postpone the procedure much more than twenty-four hours. A study of the Mississippi experience found that after August 1992, when the delay law took effect, 53 percent more women had abortions in the second trimester. If a Mississippi woman sought a procedure in a neighboring state, where she could avoid the mandatory-delay law, the second-trimester rate increased by only 8 percent. An analysis of the Mississippi law in the journal *Family Planning Perspectives* concluded, "The proportion of abortions performed later in pregnancy will probably increase if more states impose mandatory delay laws with in-person counseling requirements."[10] Mississippi is also an interesting state to examine because it has one of the toughest parental-consent laws. A pregnant Mississippi teenager is required to obtain the written consent of *both* parents to have an abortion. The law went into effect in 1993, one year after the state's mandatory-delay law. A study found little change in the number of teens getting abortions. But there was a big change in *when* they got them: the second-trimester abortion rate increased by 19 percent among teens.[11]

Texas has also moved to delay abortions whenever it can. One study of the Texas parental-notification law, enacted in 2000, found that seventeen year olds actually had fewer abortions as a result. This would seem to be good news, especially since seventeen year olds are the minors with the highest pregnancy rate and the group on which parental-consent laws have the greatest impact. However, a closer analysis by the same researchers who had previously studied the Mississippi experience found "a substantial spike" in second-trimester abortions among eighteen year olds. It seemed that many pregnant seventeen year olds in Texas simply decided to wait until they were eighteen, and legally adults, to get an abortion. As the researchers explain, "This suggests that the law induces minors who conceive a few months before their 18th birthday to delay the termination."[12] Forcing women later into pregnancy appears to be a cunning pro-life strategy. After all, in a place like Texas, abortions after sixteen weeks can be performed only at ambulatory surgical centers or hospitals—and not many of these provide abortions.[13]

As a result, many of those teens who waited until adulthood also had to leave the state for their abortion. A similar trend has been observed in Minnesota and Missouri. After these states enacted parental-consent laws, second-trimester abortions among teens increased in both states, by 18 percent and 27 percent, respectively.[14]

Another barrier to early abortion is money. Here again the pro-life side has assiduously erected hurdles. The Hyde Amendment, named for its sponsor, Republican congressman Henry Hyde, bans the use of public funds for abortion, meaning that poor women who rely on Medicaid to pay their health bills can't get this governmental insurance program to pay for an abortion. Indeed, half of women who had an abortion after sixteen weeks say pro-life restrictions were the cause, including needing time "to raise money" to pay for the procedure.[15]

In the war of words, these kinds of outcomes may provide a strategic advantage to pro-lifers. The pro-life side is able to say that it quite reasonably favors involving parents in this important decision, and it endorses a mere twenty-four-hour waiting period for reflection. In reality, these small barriers have a significant effect, not in reducing the number of abortions, but in creating more later-term abortions. It is perhaps convenient for pro-lifers who, it seems, prefer to rail against late-term abortions rather than prevent them.

Situations like these reveal the principles that guide these different movements. In the logic of the pro-life movement there is simply no distinction between the latest abortion and the earliest, no difference between a twenty-four-week-old fetus and a fertilized egg just implanted in the womb. Pro-choicers have a different view, and since at least *Roe v. Wade*, most Americans have agreed with it. For pro-choicers, pregnancy takes place along a kind of ladder. Above a certain level—twenty-four weeks—abortion is almost never permitted; below that level it is. This is a moral gradation as well as a legal one, and it is deeply ingrained in those of us who espouse the pro-choice point of view. We make a distinction between a few cells that haven't yet been implanted in a woman's uterus and a six-month-old fetus that might live outside the womb. In abortion, earlier is better. It's because of this belief that the pro-choice movement has almost single-handedly provided women the ability to act at the earliest possible moment, when a pregnancy is little more than a group of a few cells. Before the relegalization of abortion in 1973, one in four abortions took place in the second trimester of pregnancy.[16] Today, that number is one in eight.[17] Currently, 88 percent of abortions in the United States take place in the first trimester of pregnancy.[18]

Despite wide acknowledgment that with abortion, earlier is always safer, for more than a decade the pro-choice movement had to fight staunch pro-life resistance to the abortion method that allows women to end a pregnancy at the earliest moment. That method is medication abortion. Commonly known as RU-486, it is available in more than twenty-nine countries.[19] For decades, millions of women worldwide have used it safely. In the United States this method is called Mifeprex. (The French manufacturers of RU-486 were unwilling to distribute their product in the United States for fear of pro-life violence, so it is distributed by a new company formed for the exclusive purpose of marketing the drug in the United States.) With all other methods of abortion, a woman must wait approximately seven weeks after her last menstrual period. But Mifeprex, which depends on the action of a pill rather than a surgical intervention, allows women to end a pregnancy as early as four weeks after her last menstrual period (usually meaning she's really only two weeks pregnant). At this stage, the embryo is about the size of the letter T as it appears here on this page.

In 2000, after years of struggle, the pro-choice movement succeeded in getting Mifeprex considered by the FDA, which, after extensive review, approved it for distribution. A sad footnote to the pro-life movement's success in keeping Mifeprex out of the United States for years is that U.S. doctors were prevented from studying its other potential uses, like treating many of the most fatal forms of cancer.[20] (As long ago as 1993, the Institute of Medicine of the National Academies of Science, the government's scientific advisers, released a report on the potential life-saving medical uses of RU-486, stating, "Potential benefits of RU-486, other anti-progestins are extensive.")[21] Today, U.S. medical researchers are making up for lost time, exploring Mifeprex's potential in treating breast cancer, Cushing's syndrome, endometriosis, glaucoma, meningiomas, ovarian cancer, prostate cancer, uterine fibroids, brain tumors, and even bipolar depression.[22] With breast cancer alone, it is believed that Mifeprex presents the opportunity to treat 40 percent of all tumors.[23]

Unfortunately, this new research may never reach fruition. The proposed RU-486 Suspension and Review Act of 2005, legislation that originated in the offices of the pro-life Concerned Women for America, would remove this earliest abortion method from the market indefinitely.[24] The reason for wanting a ban, say pro-life groups, is that this simple medication is unsafe. With pro-life groups, supposed "safety" concerns have become one typical way to advance an ideological agenda.

After all, the facts suggest that this early abortion method is extremely safe. Of more than 350,000 American women who have used this drug since 2000, less than 1 percent have had a complication.[25] The likelihood of death resulting from a medication abortion is 0.00085 percent,[26] or less than 1 in 100,000. Compare this to the risk of dying during childbirth, which is 1 in 2,500.[27] If every drug with a complication rate of less than 1 percent and a fatality rate of less than one-ten-thousandth of 1 percent was removed from the market, very few medications in the United States would be available. There have been five deaths in the United States of women who taken medication abortion, including one that made news. Holly Patterson, a seventeen year old from California, died in 2003. The loss of their daughter led her parents to join the campaign by pro-life groups to ban Mifeprex. The death of Holly Patterson is a tragedy, but the FDA investigation of the five deaths, including hers, concluded that a causal relationship between the drug and these deaths could not be established.[28]

In the case of Mifeprex, it's difficult to see the pro-life concerns with safety as anything but a political ploy. Abortion is one of the safest medical procedures performed in the United States, with less than 1 percent risk of major complication,[29] though, as the pro-life movement well knows, risks do escalate later in pregnancy. For every 1 million abortions performed in the United States at eight weeks or earlier, there is one death. That figure rises almost fortyfold, to 1 in 29,000, after sixteen weeks of pregnancy, and a hundredfold, to 1 in 11,000, after twenty-one weeks.[30] Forcing abortions to take place later in a pregnancy, one effect of the pro-life agenda, almost guarantees that the number of complications and deaths will rise. Of course, if that happens, those who oppose abortion get to say, "See, abortion is unsafe."

The pro-life movement does have a solution to unwanted pregnancy. It is like the just-say-no campaign against drugs—the monumentally unsuccessful program of a previous fundamentalist president. The pro-life movement argues, "Just say no to sex until marriage." (This ignores the fact that many abortions, just like unwanted pregnancies, happen to married women too—nearly 1 in 5 women having an abortion in the United States is married. But put that aside for a moment.) Abstinence for the unmarried may sound like a lovely solution. Clearly, in the religious-tinged, pro-life view, it's more than a solution to the abortion problem. It's an admirable alternative lifestyle, one in which only those who are married have sex and the sex they have is with the goal of creating a family. Nearly $1 billion in federal and state matching funds has been spent since 1996 on programs that promote chastity until marriage; these programs are directed mainly at teens.[31]

Promoting abstinence has been deemed so important to some that, in the service of this cause, it's been deemed okay to fill kids' heads with half-truths and even untruths. Abstinence programs have at times equated sex with disease, depression, even death. Some programs have even tried to convince kids that condoms don't work so that abstinence seems their only option.

Some advocates may justify the lies if they effectively discourage teens from having sex. Call it collateral damage for a good cause. After all, there's nothing wrong with encouraging kids to delay sex. Perhaps even those who aren't pro-life may forgive the lies if they worked. The problem is that abstinence programs don't work. Like many pro-life initiatives, they backfire. Take, for instance, virginity-pledge programs, a main type of abstinence-only program. They are a colossal failure. In these programs, kids publicly promise to stay chaste until marriage. (If they don't happen to be virgins going in, they can, by declaring their pure intent, get a second chance. Virginity, it turns out, is a state of mind.)

These programs, it should be acknowledged, do lead teens to abstain from intercourse for, on average, eighteen months longer than teens not in similar programs. And that's impressive. In the teen years, eighteen months is a big chunk of time. Yet, it's worth noting, those eighteen intercourse-free months are a special time, and not exactly what the pro-life sponsors had in mind. A major study of some 2,500 "virgin pledgers" showed that the kids who pledge to abstain from having intercourse don't abstain from sex. They just have other kinds of sex. Virginity pledgers have porn-star sex (though porn stars appear more likely to use protection). These "virgins" are six times more likely to have oral sex than non-pledgers, and male "virgins" are four times more likely to have anal sex than those who do not take the pledge.[32]

The study, conducted by researchers at Yale and Columbia Universities, also found that these teens are far less likely to use protection in the sex they're having. It seems that having sex has been so tinged with disapproval that a teen can't plan for it. It becomes fraught with emotion, impulsive. So when they break the pledge, as 88 percent do, they are less likely to use protection than non-pledgers.[33]

Thus, while the pro-lifers hail virginity pledges because of the eighteen-month delay in intercourse, they conveniently leave out the sex-at-all-costs atmosphere that seems to result, including the anal, oral, and bareback that the same researchers have discovered.

They also fail to mention that the "virgins" have the same rate of sexually transmitted disease as their peers who do not pledge. Sadly, those "virgins" who catch STDs are also less likely to seek medical testing and treatment, and are more likely to transmit STDs to others and face serious health consequences themselves.[34]

In Arizona, when researchers studied youths in an abstinence-only program they found that 47 percent planned to have sex within the next year; 55 percent said they would before high school graduation; and, in worse news for abstainers, 57 percent planned to have sex before being in a serious relationship.[35] The pledge is clearly time limited: 80 percent of these Arizona kids told researchers they hoped to have sex before the age of twenty. Evaluators of Arizona's four-year experience with abstinence-only issued a categorical warning: "Sexual behavior rates do not appear to be changing."[36]

In Minnesota, the Department of Health commissioned a study of the state's Education Now and Babies Later abstinence-only program. Alarmingly, it found that at three schools sexual activity actually doubled among junior high school students after they participated in the abstinence program. It was as if the program acted as an aphrodisiac. Within just one year, the number of participants who said they would "probably" have sex during high school nearly doubled as well. With the exception of some promising effects on parent-teen communication, the study found no positive impact of the program on teen sexual behavior.[37]

The truth is that half of all teens between fifteen and nineteen are sexually active in the United States.[38] Whether kids attend abstinence-only programs or not, they appear equally likely to have sex. Abstinence-only programs offer the worst of both worlds: kids are not convinced about chastity, yet are completely uninformed about protection, which the programs refuse to teach.

Take the example of Pennsylvania. When that state reviewed its abstinence-only programs it found that girls in one were having sex at a much higher rate (42 percent) than girls in comprehensive sex-ed programs (27 percent). In comprehensive sex-ed programs, abstinence is encouraged. But kids are also given accurate information about contraception and disease prevention. In one county researchers noted that any positive attitudes toward abstinence declined significantly by about ninth grade, that is, at puberty, and there was a "concomitant increase in the proportion of young people who experienced sexual intercourse for the first time. Unfortunately," the researchers added, "only about half of these sexually active youth used any form of contraception." Why didn't they use contraception? The kids in the abstinence-only classes apparently didn't know much about it. The evaluators report, "Youth expressed frustration with the lack of information regarding contraception. They . . . expected reliable information. Instead, they heard mostly about the potential failures of condoms."[39]

Across the states, many reviewers raised similar concerns. Their views can be summarized in the words of one, who concluded:

> The evidence from this evaluation indicates that even if the most effective [abstinence-only] programs are replicated and the proportion of sexually abstinent youth increases, a substantial proportion of youth will continue to become sexually active before graduation from high school in every Pennsylvania community. . . . For those youth who do not remain abstinent the reduction of teen pregnancy, STDs, and HIV/AIDS requires an alternative strategy.[40]

It hardly seems likely that an alternative strategy will emerge from the federal government, now run by the abstainer-in-chief. Before George W. Bush took over the presidency in 2000, he had already sunk large sums of public monies into abstinence-only programs. As governor of Texas he'd spent $10 million on such programs.[41] Yet today, Texas is one of the more dangerous places in the country to be uneducated about safe sex. Texas has the fourth-largest population of people living with HIV/AIDS in the United States.[42]

Despite the high stakes and hefty sums, Texas managed to keep most of its students in the dark about protection. Few, for instance, seemed to know about the effectiveness of condoms. Indeed, Texas students reported to Human Rights Watch investigators reviewing the programs that they were completely unaware of how to protect themselves against STDs other than abstinence. One sixteen-year-old Texas girl concluded, "I don't know any other way but abstinence to prevent HIV." Another teen, when asked whether he had learned how to prevent HIV, replied, "Other than abstinence? No."

In Texas, the abstinence-only dogma is virtually omnipresent. All employees in one Texas school district, including bus drivers and janitors, were required to participate in abstinence-only training based on the notion that students might talk with employees other than teachers about their sex lives. One teacher reported to Human Rights Watch investigators having confiscated condoms found in students' possession. When the students asked, "Why are you taking condoms away? Shouldn't we be using condoms?" the teacher replied that he couldn't discuss it and advised that students speak with their parents.[43]

But in Texas, talking to your parents may not have been a viable option. Abstinence-only programs, not content with their control of school curricula, set their sights on undermining the advice teens receive from their parents. In fact, radio and television ads attacked parents who had strayed from the abstinence-only message. One ad posited, "In 10 seconds, you'll hear this father spread a lie. He's a good dad who is trying to help his son. But if he doesn't know the truth, he can't tell the truth." On the screen appear the words "HERE COMES THE LIE," and a father's voice says, "They'll keep you safe. They'll keep you safe. They'll keep you safe." The announcer's voice then says, "Condoms will not protect people from many sexually transmitted diseases and you could be spreading lies to your children." Sadly, many kids concluded that they didn't need condoms since they believed they "don't work."[44]

By the end of Bush's term as governor in 2000, Texas ranked dead last in the nation, fiftieth out of fifty, in the decline of teen birthrates among fifteen- to seventeen-year-old females. (Overall, the teen pregnancy rate in Texas during Bush's term as governor was one of the highest in the nation, exceeded by only four other states, including Florida—which his brother governed, using the same approach.)[45]

When Bush became president, he boldly took the dead-last approach and prescribed it for the rest of the nation. But he did so with one crucial change. Unable to develop effective abstinence-only programs, the Bush administration did the next best thing: it changed how effectiveness was assessed. Previously, quantifiable measures had been used, such as the birthrate for female participants. Unfortunately, as in Texas, this measure suggested problems with the program's effectiveness. With such stats proving inconvenient, the administration decided to track other measures of effectiveness, such as participants' attendance and their attitudes—or, as one government document described it, the "proportion of partici-pants who indicate understanding of the social, psychological, and health gains to be realized by abstaining from premarital sexual activity."[46]

It's no surprise to learn that a 2001 review of scientific evidence concluded that "adolescents' sexual beliefs, attitudes, and even in-tentions are . . . weak proxies for actual behaviors."[47] A federal government–funded report identifies two "hallmarks of good evalu-ation" in programs designed to reduce teen pregnancy rates: as-sessments that "measure behaviors, not just attitudes and beliefs," and "long-term follow-up (of at least one year)."[48]

The Bush administration's measures of abstinence-only pro-grams contain no assessments of things like actual behavior or health outcomes and do not require any minimum follow-up pe-riod. Their performance measures seem designed to produce the appearance that scientific evidence supports abstinence-only pro-grams. In fact, the best evidence does not.

Worse, the administration has attacked programs that actually work—in particular, if it deems the ideology suspect. Indeed, the Centers for Disease Control and Prevention (CDC) had a batch of curricula in what it called "programs that work," which were scien-tifically proven effective in reducing risky sexual behaviors "that contribute to HIV and other STD infections and unintended preg-nancy." Unfortunately, they were comprehensive sex-ed curricula; none were abstinence-only. At the request of "higher-ups" within the Bush administration, in 2003 the CDC removed all information about these "programs that work" from its Web site.[49] Instead, the CDC was directed to contemplate the wisdom of abstinence. Ac-cording to the Union of Concerned Scientists, top staff scientists at the CDC were required to attend a daylong session on the "science of abstinence." As one scientist who left a high-ranking CDC position reported, "Out of the entire session, conducted by a nonscientist, the only thing resembling science was one study reportedly in progress and another not even begun." Although there were no data showing abstinence-only was an effective message, CDC scientists were "regularly reminded to push the administration's abstinence-only stance."[50]

Not content to stop there, the administration decided to deliver its message more forcefully. In 2004, OMB Watch, a watchdog group that monitors the decisions of the White House Office of Management and Budget, published two reports on intimidation by the Bush administration against those who made the mistake of championing comprehensive sex education for teenagers. Take Advocates for Youth, a national group that favors comprehensive sex education. In 2001, the *Washington Post* published a leaked e-mail from the Department of Health and Human Services (HHS) in which Advocates for Youth was described by the agency as "ardent critics of the Bush administration."[51] What the group's president, James Wagoner, had said in the summer of 2003 was that abstinence-only programs "censor young people's access to information about the health benefits of contraception."[52] Soon after Wagoner's statement, his organization, which had received federal funding for fifteen years, was hit with its third HHS audit in a single year. The two previous audits had found no wrongdoing.[53] As Wagoner notes, "If they can't bury our heads in the sand about abstinence-only, they're going to try to bury our organizations in audits."[54] The Sexuality Information and Education Council of the United States (SIECUS), another national comprehensive sex-education group, was audited three times in 2003. As with the other audits, no wrongdoing was found.[55]

Even if virginity pledges and other no-sex-until-marriage programs don't work, they do serve another purpose. They have stuffed the pro-life movement full of taxpayer dollars. One in four dollars in the 2004 federal budget earmarked for abstinence-until-marriage programs went to pro-life groups.[56] Even more money is on the horizon. Indeed, the Bush administration requested $206 million in funding for abstinence-until-marriage programs just for 2006, more than double what was spent in fiscal year 2002.[57]

Lately, the abstinence movement is often the pro-life movement acting as federally sanctioned "educators." As such, they have unfettered access to our kids to promote inaccurate, flawed lessons. Focus on the Family is one of the pro-life groups behind the no-sex-until-marriage movement. Its founder, Dr. James Dobson, has called sex the "hydrogen bomb that permits the destruction of things as they are and a simultaneous reconstruction of the new order."[58]

Starting in 1992, Focus on the Family ran an ad titled "In Defense of a Little Virginity" in more than five hundred newspapers in the United States. Though it's difficult to know what a "little" virginity is, the group's strategy was to promote it as a positive, spiritually restorative cause. In doing so, it not only pushed a positive message of spiritual and sexual redemption but, inevitably, attacked sex outside of marriage as both sinful and unsafe. Indeed, much of its energy seemed to go toward a fire-and-brimstone appeal designed to convince people that safe sex was a dangerous myth. Comprehensive sex educators were derided as "condom promoters," and condoms were attacked as meaningless protection, a devilish trick of the condom pusher. To "prove" this claim, the group's ads distorted the facts. The ad cited a study of latex, and noted that the AIDS virus is small enough to pass through tiny gaps in the material. What the ad didn't say was that the study was of latex *gloves,* which are very different from latex condoms. Condoms are double-dipped in latex. And in any event, according to a study cited by the CDC, a condom (even of the poorest quality) reduces the chance of exposure to the AIDS virus 10,000 times compared to using nothing at all.[59]

The Abstinence Clearinghouse is an offshoot of the pro-life movement that refers to those who believe in comprehensive sex education as the "safe sex cartel" and "condom pushers."[60] Its mission is "to promote the appreciation for and practice of sexual abstinence [purity]" through distribution of abstinence-only publications.[61] Its Web site boasts a "medical advisory board" composed of health professionals who will not prescribe contraceptives to unmarried teens.[62] Abstinence Clearinghouse founder Leslee Unruh has close ties to the pro-life establishment. She spent most of the eighties protesting outside abortion clinics and encouraging people to protest outside the homes of physicians who provide abortions.[63] She also started a "crisis pregnancy center" in Sioux Falls, South Dakota, for which there were so many complaints that the governor had her investigated. Unruh pleaded no contest to unlicensed adoption and foster care practices as part of a plea bargain in which nineteen charges, including four felonies, were dropped. The charges resulted from Unruh's promises to pay teenagers if they remained pregnant so she could put their babies up for adoption. Tim Wilka, one of the state's attorneys at the time, explained, "There were so many allegations about improper adoptions being made [against her] and how teenage girls were being pressured to give up their children," he says. "Governor George Mickelson called me and asked me to take the case."[64]

Despite the wealth and abundant political connections of the pro-life movement's abstinence-only wing, the majority of the American public do not want their children taught abstinence-only. According to a 2004 poll conducted by National Public Radio, only 30 percent of American adults believe that the government should fund programs in which "abstaining from sexual activity" is the exclusive message. Sixty-seven percent believe "the money should be used to fund more comprehensive sex education programs that include information on how to obtain and use condoms and other contraceptives."[65] Not only is the federal government sanctioning abstinence-only education against most parents' wishes, but it refuses to even review the contents of the programs. We know the programs don't work. What few know is that as long as educators claim to teach abstinence, they can pretty much teach whatever they like.

When in 2004 a report titled "The Content of Federally Funded Abstinence-Only Education Programs" examined these programs, the results were startling. More than 80 percent of the abstinence-only curricula, used by more than two-thirds of federal grant recipients in 2003, contained false, misleading, or distorted information.[66] Students have been told that "5% to 10% of women who have legal abortions will become sterile"; that "premature birth, a major cause of mental retardation, is increased following an abortion of the first pregnancy"; that "tubal and cervical pregnancies are increased following abortions";[67] and that "women are more prone to suicide [after abortion]."[68] No research supports these claims.

The congressional report revealed that "erroneous statements are presented as proven scientific facts."[69] For instance, one abstinence-only curriculum claims the "theory" that condoms help prevent the spread of STDs "is not supported by the data."[70] That same curriculum tells kids that "in heterosexual sex, condoms fail to prevent HIV approximately 31% of the time."[71] It also falsely—why not?—lets kids know that the exchange of "sweat and tears are risk factors for HIV transmission."[72] One can only imagine how traumatic P.E. class is once you've been told that. The report concluded that "although the curricula purport to provide scientifically accurate information about contraceptive failure rates, many exaggerate these failure rates, providing affirmatively false or misleading information that misstates the effectiveness of various contraceptive methods in preventing disease transmission or pregnancy."[73] Why, in other words, use a condom when you've been taught that pregnancy will occur one out of every seven times you do? Or that HIV will be transmitted one out of every three times?

Also alarming in the abstinence-only curricula is the subtle and not-so-subtle view of women that is communicated. The pro-choice movement has struggled, and largely succeeded, in convincing a generation of women they too can be professionals and self-supporters as well as mothers. Abstinence-only curricula inform their young students, male and female, that women need "financial support," whereas men need "admiration"; "women gauge their happiness and judge their success on their relationships," whereas "men's happiness and success hinge on their accomplishments."[74]

Pro-life groups have used their access to kids via abstinence programs not just to scare them about birth control and abortion but also to recruit them to the pro-life cause—one curriculum calls a forty-three-day embryo a "thinking person"[75]—as well as the cause of Jesus Christ. Thus, pro-life groups, now reborn as pro-abstinence groups, are using taxpayer dollars for religious indoctrination, focusing on the most impressionable people: children.

In fact, proselytizing appears to be the underlying objective of many abstinence-only programs. In 2002, a federal judge ruled that the Louisiana governor's Program on Abstinence had illegally provided funding to organizations that were advancing religion. Evidence included one abstinence group that claimed its program focused on the "virgin birth." "God," maintained this program, "desires sexual purity as a way of life." The group also stated in a monthly reporting form that "there were several young people who did not know about Joseph and Mary nor how they live for God."[76] Another group requested money from the state to purchase Bibles for participants.[77] Still another group used state money to hold prayer rallies outside abortion clinics.[78] According to the terms of the settlement, the Louisiana governor's program agreed to cease using public dollars to advance religion in any way. But in 2005, the program was charged with contempt because many of the abstinence-only programs continued to promote religious doctrine.[79]

The Silver Ring Thing, a national abstinence-only group, received more than $1 million in public funding from 2003 through 2005.[80] Its mission is to saturate the United States with a generation of young people who have taken a vow of sexual abstinence until marriage.[81] To symbolize their vow, teens agree to wear a specially inscribed silver ring—the inscription is a biblical verse. A complaint brought against the Department of Health and Human Services and the agency within it that oversees grants to abstinence-only programs charges that the federal government, by funding the group, improperly used public money to promote religion. The complaint states, "The Silver Ring thing is a ministry that uses abstinence education as a means to bring 'unchurched' students to Jesus Christ."[82]

In a British Broadcasting Corporation (BBC) documentary, *American Virgins,* Silver Ring Thing executive director Dennis Pattyn explained what motivates him. "I believe that the end of the world is approaching very quickly and I believe that Christ will come back," he said.[83] The BBC reporter seemed surprised. If the end of the world is so close, then should we be all that worried about abstinence? Pattyn didn't miss a beat. "We're not really putting our energy into abstinence as much as we're putting it into faith," he explained. "Abstinence is the tool that we're using to reach children."[84]

For those looking for considered answers on how to navigate the sexual pressures of adolescence, you'd better buckle your seat belts. Sexual dalliance, like a failure to accept Christ, leads to a bumpy ride straight to hell and courtesy, these days, of taxpayer dollars. "In hell non-believers will be doomed to exist in unending torment with the Devil and his demons. . . . [N]onbelievers will spend eternity in agony," Silver Ring Thingers learn. If you have chosen to reject Christ, then your final destination will be the lake of fire.[85] In August 2005, in response to the complaint over inappropriate use of taxpayer money, the Department of Health and Human Services suspended funding to the group.[86]

Abstinence-only programs tend to have a regional concentration. School districts in the South are almost five times more likely than in the Northeast to teach only abstinence.[87] The evidence suggests that this may help create another crisis . . . for the South. After all, southern states have the highest rate of new HIV/AIDS infections, the highest rate of STDs, as well as the highest rate of teen births.[88] Whereas new cases of AIDS decreased or remained constant in the Northeast, Midwest, and West in one recent period, the South, alone, experienced an increase.[89] Of the estimated new AIDS cases in 2001, 46 percent were in the South. Seven of the ten states with the highest chlamydia rates, all of the states with the highest rates of gonorrhea, and nine of the top ten states for syphilis rates are all in the South.[90] So troubling was this trend that HIV/AIDS experts convened in 2003 to write "The Southern States Manifesto HIV/SIDS & STDs in the South: A Call to Action." They opened their document mincing no words: "There is an emergency under-way in the southern states of the United States. There is a pressing need to address the unique epidemics of HIV, AIDS and STDs in the south and their disparate impact on southern citizens."[91]

What is so frustrating about the current vogue for abstinence-only programs is that we already know what works to combat the crisis of teen pregnancy (as well as the emergency of sexually trans-mitted disease, which is linked to it). In 2001, UNICEF conducted a survey of teenage birthrates in the industrialized world—it wanted to figure out why some rich countries have teenage birthrates that are ten or fifteen times higher than others. The United States ranks number one for teen moms, far outpacing the rest of the industrial-ized world—four times the European Union average and 60 per-cent higher than the rate in the United Kingdom, which came in second.[92] In the twenty-eight countries under review, there were 760,000 births to teenagers, two-thirds of which occurred in the United States.[93] The United States is so bad in preventing teen pregnancy that it is the only rich nation smack in the middle of the

Third World block for teen births—ranking just behind Thailand and directly before Rwanda.[94]

Some countries have successfully reversed this trend. The Netherlands, for example, has reduced its teenage birthrate by a staggering 72 percent in thirty years while also having the lowest teenage abortion rates in the industrialized world.[95] UNICEF reports, "In general, studies of the Dutch experience have concluded that the underlying reason for success has been the combination of a relatively inclusive society with more open attitudes toward sex and sex education, including contraception."[96] A 1994 international conference called "Can We Learn from the Dutch?" concluded that young people in the Netherlands "feel comfortable discussing sexuality in a warm, mutually supporting atmosphere" in which "requests for contraceptive services are not associated with shame or embarrassment" and in which "the media is willing to carry explicit messages designed for young people about contraceptive services." The result is that teenagers who are having sex in the Netherlands see using contraception "as ingrained as not going through a red light."[97] Interestingly, the Dutch approach has led not to a sex-indulgent teenage culture, but rather, as the report concludes, to a "higher average age at first intercourse."[98]

Another country that successfully reduced its teenage birthrate is Sweden. UNICEF reports that beginning in 1975 Sweden "radically reviewed its school sex-education curriculum. Abstinence and sex-only-within-marriage were dropped. Contraceptive education was made an explicit part of the school curriculum, and a nationwide network of youth clinics was established to provide confidential advice and free contraceptives to young people."[99] In the same year, the abortion law was changed to allow termination of pregnancy free of charge. The Swedes took a practical, nonjudgmental approach to their teenagers' sexuality, considering it "neither as desirable nor undesirable, but as inevitable—this being the case, teenagers' use of contraceptives is viewed as highly desirable because it will prevent both childbearing and abortion."[100] As a result of these changes, Sweden has nearly half the teen abortion rate than that of the United States (17.7 versus 30.2 per 1,000 teens).[101]

Unfortunately, there seems little chance that the United States will move in the direction of encouraging teens to use contraception, or implementing any of the other methods that have actually reduced teen pregnancies and, thereby, abortions. After all, the Bush administration not only likes to fund hell-fearing cheerleaders for abstinence but even puts them in charge. Under Bush's presidency, abstinence-only advocates have been rewarded with appointments to outlandishly inappropriate posts. Many of those appointments have been made to the powerful Department of Health and Human Services, initially run by pro-lifer Tommy Thompson, whose own political strategist described the Department as "ground zero for the ideological wars in this country."[102] One of HHS's crucial positions for women's reproductive health is the Office of Population Affairs, which runs the nation's Title X program. Title X's mission is to provide contraceptive services to low-income people and conduct research on teen sex issues.

Each year, approximately 4 million women rely on Title X clinics around the country for contraception.[103] The vast majority of these women (71 percent) are unmarried.[104] In 2002, Thompson put in charge of this program Dr. Alma Golden, who ran an abstinence-only group out of Texas.[105] Much of Dr. Golden's lifework until then had been aimed at discouraging unmarried people from having sex. In her present position, she is charged with providing them with contraception. It would seem that Dr. Golden, and her abstinence-until-marriage philosophy, was chosen specifically to *not* lead the agency, at least in its assigned mission.

It should come as little surprise that the Title X budget has remained stagnant, even though the number of patients it serves has swollen.[106] The federal government currently spends nearly equal amounts of money promoting abstinence-only programs and the Title X program.[107] Not surprisingly, Dr. Golden's most noteworthy acts in her position overseeing the office have been defending abstinence-only programs against the sea of evidence that they are ineffective.[108]

Golden seems profoundly unsuited for her job, and the inevitable result no doubt is more teen pregnancies and more teen abortions. Perhaps this ought to trouble even pro-lifers. But the truth is that the abstinence-only set takes a different view. Once the virgin lapses, once the abstainer indulges, he or she might as well hurry off to the lake of fire. As a spokesman for the abstinence-only group True Love Waits explained, "If you're talking about a person who is not going to keep the [abstinence] pledge anyway, whether or not they would use contraception isn't really something that concerns us. Waiting is what we're striving for here."[109]

chapter four

The Condom Hoax

IN 1993, DR. SUSAN WELLER of the University of Texas Medical Branch made a mistake. Actually, she made a series of mistakes, packaged in one neat document. She'd set out to review the available studies on the condom. Her intent was to gauge the effectiveness of this simple latex sleeve in preventing the spread of HIV. At the time, Weller thought she'd come up with some shocking results. She found that when "discordant" couples (one person HIV positive, the other HIV negative) had sex, condoms were only 69 percent effective in reducing the risk of HIV transmission.[1] The news seemed ominous. If you had sex with someone who had the HIV virus, a condom wasn't much protection at all; 31 percent of the time you risked contracting the virus.

The problem was her study was wrong. She admits to this now, and even refers to it as having a "flawed study design."[2] The Department of Health and Human Services and the Centers for Disease Control and Prevention released a statement to set the record straight, explaining her analytical blunders.[3] For one thing, she combined couples who *always* used a condom with couples who *sometimes* used a condom, which is a little like measuring the effectiveness of seat belts by studying injuries sustained by seat-belt wearers and non-seat-belt wearers alike.

This was Weller's first published work in the field of condom research, and she has since published reviews of condom effectiveness that are considered the accepted data for the field. But that first mistake lives on.

The pro-choice movement long ago made a fundamental decision. It has been the realistic movement. And if, as a result, it has given up the high ground of deeply felt, religiously intoned "values," it has gained something else. It has science. The deep desire to know and manage the world (and give us each a chance to manage our own little worlds) through science has been the great urge of pro-choicers from at least the advent of the birth control pill. This belief—or value—has led to a willingness to follow the evidence wherever it leads. Pro-choicers have signed on to science, and in doing so they've agreed that it is evidence that reveals the truth—a truth that is knowable and usable, not mysterious and withheld.

The pro-life movement, by contrast, has been less keen on the truth that science can yield. When science and faith clash, it sides with faith. For pro-lifers, condom use, like contraception, is simply anathema. Abstinence is the acceptable form of safe sex. To advance this goal, they're willing to trounce good science, or make up their own. Yet, lately, the pro-life movement has been avid about casting the *appearance* of science on its faith-based beliefs.

And so Dr. Weller's first flawed study played right into their hands. Faulty science can be corrected in the course of scientific inquiry. But when bad science finds a friend in religious fundamentalism, all bets are off. Indeed, Weller's first mistake spun out of her control almost instantly. The pro-life movement not only opposes abortion and the birth control pill. It doesn't much like the lowly condom. And it quickly put Weller's flawed study to work as one weapon with which to attack condom education in schools and in public policy across the globe.

The pro-life movement has insisted on using Weller's faulty data despite the, by now, well-known facts. As the Centers for Disease Control has found, "Latex condoms provide an essentially impermeable barrier to particles the size of STD pathogens [which includes HIV]."[4] The National Institutes of Health, the Department of Health and Human Services, and the National Institute of Allergy and Infectious Diseases jointly stated in 2001 that "consistent use of male condoms protects against HIV transmission between women and men" and that "the data provide strong evidence for the effectiveness of condoms for reducing sexually transmitted HIV."[5] Using a condom during sex is 10,000 times safer than not using one.[6] This is good news to most everyone except the abstinence-only, pro-life crowd. This group apparently fears that the availability of effective disease-prevention methods will undermine its larger agenda, promoting a world in which people are either abstinent or making babies. If one of your goals is to encourage aspiring virgins to stick to their pledges, lofty purity ideals are fine and dandy. But scaring the bejesus out of people helps too. (Religious-based movements have long understood that the promise of heaven is more potent when teamed with the threat of hellfire.) And so the pro-life movement leads a stupefying and aggressive pseudoscientific campaign against the condom.

In this campaign, almost all of the "scientific" claims are based on research that's wrong, taken out of context, or distorted. And some pro-lifers, though they should know better, still continue to cite Weller's study. Abstinence groups broadcast the bad news to children. One such group, Me, My World, My Future, introduces its argument this way: "A meticulous review of condom effectiveness was reported by Dr. Susan Weller in 1993." Then, having set up the supposed "scientificness" of the evidence, the group's curriculum cites that scary 69 percent statistic. Another curriculum, Why kNOw, cites Dr. Weller's data and then cuts quickly to the frightening part: "In heterosexual sex, condoms fail to prevent HIV approximately 31 percent of the time." One out of three times you're risking your life, the abstinence gurus seem to imply. These curricula say flatly and falsely that HIV and other pathogens can "pass through" condoms. One curriculum, taking a cinematic view of science, instructs students to "think on a microscopic level. . . . Any imperfections in the contraceptives not visible to the eye, could allow sperm, STI [sexually transmitted infection], or HIV to pass through." If this fantastic voyage isn't enough, the same curriculum warns, "The actual ability of condoms to prevent the transmission of HIV/AIDS even if the product is intact, is not definitively known."[7]

The intrepid anti-condom campaign proceeds as if no one had done any real work in this area. Groups such as Pro-Life America (its Web site proclaims, "Condom Warnings: Beware!"),[8] United for Life (its Web site wonders, "Could Condoms Leak HIV?"),[9] the Heritage House ("Condoms: Do They Really Work?"),[10] Human Life International ("How the Condom Fails at Preventing Transmission of the HIV Virus"),[11] Physicians for Life ("'Safe Sex' Is a Deadly Game"),[12] the National Association of Catholic Families ("Condoms—a Step in the Wrong Direction"),[13] and Concerned Women for America ("Medical Diagnosis: Condoms Are Full of Holes"),[14] along with many other pro-life groups, like to assert that the use of condoms is actually *causing* the spread of HIV and other STDs. They'd like people to believe that condoms are faulty, and thus dangerous. That the faults are fictional or overstated is of little concern to them. The American Life League, in its publication "The Flawed Condom: Spotting the Big Holes in Condom Propaganda, All the facts You Need to Make an Open-and-Shut Case against the Pro-condom Crowd," claims that there is a "condom cover up."[15] Some national pro-life groups are even more active in discouraging condom use internationally, where the consequences are even more devastating. The Abstinence Clearinghouse launched "Abstinence Africa," which has a unique take on the globally accepted prevention message: "ABC." ABC stands for "**A**bstinence," "**B**e Faithful," and "Use **C**ondoms," advice accepted even by the Bush administration. As the Abstinence Clearinghouse's Web site explains: "Why settle for 'C,' when your children could have 'A' and 'B'?"[16] The Abstinence Clearinghouse Web site boasts of 350 affiliates operating to discourage condom use in African countries with the world's highest rates of HIV.[17]

In 2003, the Vatican, another believer in the condom cover-up, defended its efforts to halt condom distribution in countries ravaged by AIDS. Like its abstinence-only colleagues, the Vatican fingers the condom as one reason for the spread of AIDS. Its key document, "Family Values versus Safe Sex," was written by Alfonso Cardinal Lopez Trujillo, president of the Pontifical Council for the Family for the Vatican. It claims that "those promoting the condom without properly informing the public of its failure rates (both in its *perfect* use and in its *typical* use, and the *cumulative risks*), have led to, lead to, and will continue to lead to the death of many."[18] What was particularly interesting about the Vatican's approach was that it appeared to rely on science for outcomes that it found fulfilling for other reasons. In a rare act of journalistic doggedness, the British Broadcasting Corporation examined the evidence on which Trujillo based his claims.[19] "All told us they believe condoms are an essential component of an effective AIDS strategy and oppose the kind of general prohibition on condoms that Cardinal Trujillo advises," the BBC reported. In fact, the BBC discovered that "all the authoritative AIDS specialists cited by the Cardinal do in fact support the use of condoms against HIV."

The BBC worked with one of the scientists cited by the Vatican, Dave Lytle, a former senior researcher at the U.S. Food and Drug Administration who, in the 1980s, led an investigation on the effectiveness of condoms. "My reaction is one of disappointment," Dave Lytle told the BBC. "[Trujillo] didn't pay attention to the paper, he took a number out of it, and basically misused it." Lytle told the BBC that the laboratory conditions of his test were not comparable to those that occur during sex. For one thing, the viruses he tested were one-fifth the size of the HIV virus, which he didn't test. Also, the pressures he used to test condoms were higher than those present in the typical sex act. Based on his research experience, Lytle concluded the exact opposite of what pro-lifers want people to believe: normal intact condoms are "impermeable to HIV."

The BBC asked Lytle to review another study, one not cited by the cardinal but which is a favorite of our domestic anti-condom campaigners, such as United for Life,[20] Pro-Life America,[21] Physicians for Life,[22] and the American Life League.[23] The study was conducted by Dr. C. M. Roland, a leading specialist on rubber technology at the U.S. Naval Research Laboratory. Dr. Roland tested latex rubber film and wrote in 1998 that "small particles can pass through." He, however, did not use actual viruses, which are dangerous and difficult to handle. He used microscopic florescent beads. Unlike the other researchers, he was unwilling to speak with the BBC reporters. Lytle, confused by the results, asked to observe Roland's research technique. He then tried it out using a real virus. As Lytle explains to the BBC reporters, "We went to see his lab and then later with one of the people who did that study in our lab we used viruses." He found that none passed through. "We think the virus data should take precedence," he said.

None of the BBC's revelations have much influenced the debate in the United States. But then the anti-condom brigade appears determined to stop the spread of condoms for reasons that have little to do with the science behind them. The science, to anti-condom crusaders, is there to be manipulated.

In recent years, Tom Coburn, now a U.S. senator from Oklahoma, has brought new levels of daring to this tactic. He is described by the pro-life group called 100% Pro-Life PAC as "more than just a consistent and reliable vote on pro-life issues." Dr. Coburn is "a leader in the pro-life movement."[24] He won that reputation with positions like this: "I favor the death penalty for abortionists and other people who take life."[25]

Coburn has opened up a sneaky new front in the offensive against the condom. He claims to be very worried about the spread of HPV, the human papillomavirus. In 1999, Coburn drafted legislation mandating that condom labels state that they cannot prevent the transmission of HPV and, further, that HPV can lead to cervical cancer.

The HPV virus is common and worrisome. According to a 1997 article published in the *American Journal of Medicine*, nearly three out of four Americans between the ages of fifteen and forty-nine have been infected with genital HPV at some point in their lives.[26] Genital HPV, which can be transmitted via any skin contact (not just sexual contact), is usually harmless. Most often, the human body defends itself from HPV, and it disappears with no ill effects. Some strains, however, can lead to genital warts, which can usually be treated. Approximately ten genital HPV strains, out of seventy, are present in cervical cancer in women[27] (though just having one of those strains doesn't mean you'll get cervical cancer).

Although HPV is common in the United States, cervical cancer is relatively rare, with about 13,000 new cases per year.[28] And though Coburn and his supporters won't publicize it, cervical cancer is actually on the decline in the United States. The reason is the introduction of the Pap smear, which can detect precancerous changes of the cervix in their earliest stages. Cervical cancer is highly preventable if detected early, which is what a Pap smear does. Since the introduction of the Pap test in the 1950s, the rate of cervical cancer has dropped precipitously—a decrease of 74 percent between 1955 and 1992.[29] Today, the majority of cases of cervical cancer are in women who have not had a Pap smear in five years or more.[30]

In 2000, at Coburn's request, the National Institutes of Health, the Food and Drug Administration, the Centers for Disease Control and Prevention, and the U.S. Agency for International Development (the agencies responsible for condom research, condom regulation, condom-use recommendations, and HIV/AIDS and STD prevention) hosted a meeting of experts to compile and exam-

ine 138 peer-reviewed papers on the effectiveness of condo
preventing the transmission of STDs. In its report, the panel explained the difficulty in making definitive conclusions based on the
available studies. For one thing, there exist ethical boundaries that
prevent the ideal studies from being conducted. Researchers cannot ask study subjects to go have sex without a condom and come
back and see what they caught. They also cannot ask those with
treatable diseases, like HPV, to remain untreated, have sex with others using a condom, and see how likely transmission was. Thus, the
NIH took the cautious route. It pointed out that given the studies
out there, it was not always possible to say with certainty that the
condom stopped everything, like, for example, HPV or chlamydia.
The condom, the group concluded, was effective in preventing
HIV transmission in men and women and gonorrhea in men. With
regard to HPV, it stated, "The panel stressed that the absence of
definitive conclusions reflected inadequacies of the evidence available and should not be interpreted as proof of the adequacy or in-
adequacy of the condom to reduce the risk of STDs."[31] In other
words, a definitive answer was not possible either way. Still, the
panel was able to conclude: "Study results did suggest that condom use might afford some reduction in risk of HPV associated
diseases, including genital warts in men and cervical neoplasia [or
cancer] in women."[32]

The panelists knew how their careful words might be construed
and explicitly cautioned anyone against using the report to discourage condom use. Panelist Dr. Edward Hook explained, "People are
turning around the findings . . . to say that to promote condoms is
incorrect. I think that's a very, very dangerous thing to do. I would
not want it on my conscience if somebody were to . . . decide not to

use condoms when they were having sex, and acquire a disease that could change their entire life, much less end it."[33]

But Coburn reacted as if the lack of definitive evidence either way on HPV prevention proved his case. Somehow he managed to conclude that the government was covering up for "condom pushers." For Coburn, the real danger was not that too few people were using this proven barrier to the transmission of at least some STDs, as scientist after scientist argued, it was that the government championed condoms for all STDs. Coburn was so incensed at what he saw as this governmental manipulation that he joined pro-life congressman Dave Weldon and anti-condom groups the Physician's Consortium and the Catholic Medical Association to call for the resignation of the director of the CDC, Dr. Jeffrey Koplan.[34] During their press conference, Congressman Weldon told reporters, "Clearly, the [Centers for Disease Control] and the proponents of 'safe sex' have overplayed the effectiveness of condoms and tens of millions of Americans are living with the consequences of decisions they made based on faulty information, much of it paid for with their tax dollars." He added, "I think there's grounds for class action suits against the government based on the report" since the government "had been promoting the use of condoms."[35]

Representatives from the CDC issued a polite rebuttal that explained that their report "doesn't say condoms are ineffective—it says the evidence is fully sufficient only for HIV and gonorrhea and for other STDs more research is needed."[36] The CDC stated that it "continues to advise that the surest protection from STDs is sexual abstinence and mutually monogamous relations with an uninfected partner."[37] For the sexually active, the CDC added, "male latex condoms, when used correctly and consistently, are highly effective in protecting against HIV and can reduce the risk of other STDs."[38]

The CDC showed restraint, and perhaps hesitation, in the face of powerful political forces. Other experts refused. In an interview with the Associated Press, Tom Broker, president of the International Papillomavirus Society, a coalition of experts that studies HPV, protested: "I want to be polite. But it appalls me when I see scientific and medical studies being manipulated for a different agenda." Broker told the Associated Press that the focus should instead be on the fact that condoms have been shown to reduce the risk of cervical cancer, which is caused by HPV.[39]

To some, this was part of a consistent theme: when science conflicts with politics, it's science that has to go. Democrats like Representative Henry Waxman charged that "information that used to be based on science is being systematically removed from the public when it conflicts with the administration's political agenda."[40] He put it this way, "Are condoms perfect? Of course not. But reality requires us . . . to ask a key question: compared to what? Some lawmakers insist that abstinence-only education is the solution to teen pregnancy and sexually transmitted diseases because abstinence works each time. Well, the evidence, however, indicates that abstinence-only education works rarely, if at all."[41]

Within months of Coburn's press conference, the CDC director indeed did step down.[42] He cited reasons other than the condom controversy for his decision. Nevertheless, the CDC soon took down information from its Web site on the effectiveness of condoms in preventing the spread of STDs and HIV, replacing it with a "fact sheet" that omits information about the different types of condoms (that novelty and lambskin condoms don't prevent the spread of HIV) and expunged information on how to use condoms effectively.[43]

President Bush rewarded Coburn for his good work by appointing him to cochair, of all things, the Presidential Advisory Council on HIV/AIDS. When it comes to preventing the spread of AIDS, Bush clearly prefers Right-thinking anti-condom crusaders to scientists. Bush also appointed Dr. Joe McIlhaney, a Texas-based abstinence advocate and another outspoken leader of the anti-condom movement, to the council. McIlhaney founded the Medical Institute for Sexual Health in 1992, the sole mission of which is to promote sex only within marriage. He was not endorsed by any reputable medical organization, but McIlhaney had demonstrated one important qualification: an adeptness at ignoring inconvenient scientific data. "Dr. McIlhaney's presentation [on HIV and AIDs] tended to report the outlier data as 'proof' that condoms don't work rather than present those reports in the context of the entire data set," concluded the Texas health commissioner. "The only data reported in the presentation are those which supported his bias on the topics he addressed."[44] This tendency, of course, aligned him with Coburn, who immediately upon his appointment "promised to challenge the national focus on condom use to prevent the spread of HIV," the Associated Press reported (no doubt with McIlhaney's help).[45] Coburn also used the announcement of his appointment to explain that the only thing that's going to work to prevent HIV/AIDS transmission is telling people they shouldn't have sex outside of marriage.

As far as Coburn's HPV concerns, it's worth noting that his proposed condom legislation did have one important effect. He wanted condom labels to carry the warning that condoms cannot stop HPV transmission or cervical cancer. In championing this bill, according to the Associated Press, "he single-handedly held up popular legislation helping uninsured women pay for cancer treatment."[46] Ironically, that legislation covered treatment of cervical cancer, the very disease he claimed to be concerned about.

For pro-lifers like Coburn and members of the movement's anti-condom wing, nothing seems capable of changing their minds. And this is part of the problem. However mired in medicine or science or safety a debate becomes, it's important to remember that the real interest is elsewhere. The pseudoscientific debate about condoms or about HPV is, for them, a debate about how they think we should all live. And no matter where the science leads, the pro-life side has an indestructible set of convictions in this regard. Indeed, this is what is so frustrating about entering an "open-minded debate" on safety or health concerns. Doctors and researchers can agree to go where the evidence leads. But pro-lifers don't sign on to these terms, even if they sometimes act as if they do. So meeting imagined safety concerns with a mountain of data is a thankless endeavor. When predetermined passions rule, medicine is powerless.

Perhaps the most scandalous example of this is in the pro-life reaction to a recent scientific breakthrough. It's been referred to as "the biggest vaccine ever,"[47] and its availability, slated as early as 2006, could eradicate HPV diseases permanently. Dr. Diane Harper, of Dartmouth Medical School, is a developer of the HPV vaccine and conducted an international clinical trial that found it is 100 percent effective against persistent HPV infections in women who followed the protocol. Its efficacy was only slightly reduced (93–95 percent effective) in those who started but did not complete the protocol. Harper said, "We believe this shows enormous potential to eradicate the great majority of cervical cancers world-wide."[48] She went further: "Preliminary findings show the vaccine may prevent all diseases associated with HPV, such as abnormal pap smears, anal cancer, vaginal cancer, vulvular cancer, esophageal cancer and even mouth and oral cancers."[49] The vaccine has no side effects, except for pain or redness at the injection site. It offers the chance to save 280,000 women worldwide each year from death caused by cervical cancer.

On the announcement of this amazing scientific achievement, one would expect the pro-life movement to join the celebration. After all, pro-lifers had been vigorously wringing their hands over the possibility that latex wouldn't protect against HPV. Instead, the pro-life movement, as has become typical, cast unsubstantiated doubts on the vaccine's safety. The movement went so far as to assert that providing protection from sexually transmitted diseases through such a vaccine would be dangerous. "Giving the HPV vaccine to young women could be potentially harmful," said Bridget Maher of the Family Research Council. And here was the unscientific reason: "They may see it as a license to engage in premarital sex," she said.[50]

Indeed, it's fair to say that, for the pro-life brigade, sexually transmitted disease isn't a scourge. Just the opposite. The pro-life campaign against the condom has always been primarily about scaring people out of a way of life, one that takes as a key tenet that people have sex for pleasure. As the American Life League puts it, the condom's "biggest flaw" is that "those using it to prevent the conception of another human being are offending God. . . . Any action, including condom use, which proposes to render procreation impossible is intrinsically evil."[51]

Leslee Unruh, president of the Abstinence Clearinghouse, chimed in against the new HPV vaccine, saying that money spent on developing the vaccine "would be much safer spent on abstinence education."[52] Scott Phelps, of the Abstinence and Marriage Education Partnership, cast doubts on the safety of the vaccine: "We're all for preventing cancer, but is this really the way to do it—by shooting stuff into our kids?" he asked. "What are the side effects in these young children? And are they told what the vaccine is for? I'd be interested to listen in on that discussion."[53] Dr. Harper, one of the HPV vaccine inventors, will certainly be given her place in history as the mother of a most-important life-saving medical advancement. She hopes for a 2006 release of the vaccine (we all should). But she may not be taking into account that a well-financed, powerfully positioned, religiously motivated, antisex movement may prefer to keep it off the market. And that movement has a résumé full of successes in keeping several other important medications from the American people.

chapter five

No Plan B

THE PRO-LIFE SIDE, as everyone knows, professes no greater desire than to reduce the number of abortions. Yet when an innovation comes along with the potential to dramatically curb the number of abortions—by one-third or even one-half—the pro-life side doesn't necessarily cheer the cause. It's the pro-choice side that has championed just such innovations. Sadly, pro-choicers have often done this in the face of deep and, lately, increasingly successful resistance by the pro-life movement.

Consider one striking example: the case of emergency contraception (EC). Not long after the birth control pill was developed in the sixties, doctors discovered its potential to prevent pregnancy if taken in higher doses soon after unprotected sex. Throughout the seventies and eighties many college campus health centers, family planning clinics, and private physicians in the know would cut up a pack of birth control pills. They'd give two pills to deeply grateful patients who had come to them panicked. The effect can be dramatic. If a woman has unprotected sex midcycle, her chance of pregnancy is 8 percent. If she takes EC within seventy-two hours, her chance of pregnancy is reduced to 2.7 percent, and if she takes it within twenty-four hours of unprotected sex, her risk of getting pregnant decreases to 0.4 percent.[1] It has long been clear that this underutilized method had the potential to reduce the unintended pregnancy rate by as much as 50 percent, and therefore, the straightforward math shows, to reduce the number of abortions in the United States by 50 percent (preventing about 700,000 per year).[2]

At first, this promising medication was called postcoital contraception. More recently, it's been known as the morning-after pill, which medical purists don't like because it can be taken on the second or even third day after unprotected sex and because it's two pills, not one. Today, it is most accurately called emergency contraception. Its commercial name is Plan B, as in what to do when Plan A (not having sex or having protected sex) fails.

Emergency contraception was available in other countries long before it broke into U.S. religious politics. In fact, more than one hundred nations have made emergency contraception available for the prevention of pregnancy, including countries that outlaw abortion such as Argentina, Brazil, Colombia, El Salvador, Kenya, Pakistan, Thailand, and Venezuela.[3] Still, through the early nineties most American doctors were unaware of its potential, and few women had heard of it. In 1992, pro-choice advocates began planning a strategy to make EC more available to American women. In 1994, the Center for Reproductive Law and Policy* filed a Citizens' Petition requesting that the FDA declare emergency contraception safe and effective. The advocacy group wanted the FDA to require pharmaceutical companies to tell consumers that emergency contraception is an acceptable use of birth control pills, and to define the dosage.[4]

*Now known as the Center for Reproductive Rights.

In response, the FDA convened an advisory panel to review emergency contraception. The panel unanimously concluded that oral contraceptives are "safe" and "effective" for use as emergency contraceptive pills. As a result of the advisory panel's recommendation, in 1997 the FDA went a step further and published a notice in the *Federal Register* about the safety of a high dose of contraception pills and, in a rare act, indicated it was prepared to accept applications for an EC product.[5] The notice was intended to encourage pharmaceutical companies to market something that would come packaged as emergency contraception with the usual instructions and warnings, something to replace the ad hoc administration of extra birth control pills. As FDA deputy commissioner Mary Pendergast explained at the time, "We hope the notice in the Federal Register will calm people's anxieties about using oral contraception as morning after pills. And we're still hopeful that someone will come forward and market them."[6]

It was assumed that some manufacturer would jump at the chance. After all, there was no costly, timely FDA approval process to go through. And what's more, there was no expensive research to do. They already had the product. Manufacturers made oral contraceptives. Wouldn't the chance to expand the market for a product they'd already developed be tantalizing? The manufacturers, though, had already been sufficiently chilled, courtesy of the pro-life movement, to the idea of distributing it in the United States. The *Wall Street Journal* reported in 1998, "American Home Products Corp. and Schering AG, which make the oral contraceptives used in the morning after pill's independent clinical trials, want no part of the drug." American Home Products executives had already met with representatives of the Family Research Council, a Washington,

D.C., pro-life group that pointedly asked executives to "clarify their views" on the product.[7] Perhaps "clarifying views" doesn't sound too threatening—except that in the context of a radicalized pro-life movement, clarification is often the first step to protest, boycott, and even violence. (Searle is just one corporation that has been the subject of pro-life protests. Its sin? Manufacturing birth control pills.) Responsible corporate officers are acutely aware of the threats posed by the pro-life ideology. How could they not be? Over the past twenty-five years there have been no fewer than 140,000 incidents of violence and disruption under the banner of the pro-life cause, including 7 murders, 17 attempted murders, 41 bombings, 172 arsons, 373 invasions, 3 kidnappings, 1,141 vandalisms, 100 butric-acid attacks, 655 anthrax threats, 139 assaults, 365 death threats, 474 stalkings, 605 bomb threats, and 10,666 hate mails and harassing calls.[8] Was it any surprise that conservative company officials balked at entering this new fray? "They [American Home Products executives] assured us they have no intention" of marketing it, Gracie Hsu, a satisfied Family Research Council policy analyst, told the *Journal*.[9]

Schering apparently felt caught. Spokeswoman Wendy Neininger explained, "It's not an easy question and never has been. One segment of society is holding a product hostage. Another part of society wants to force companies to produce a product that they don't want to produce." Schering, too, decided against marketing emergency contraception in the United States, even though, in 1997, it had sold close to a million units of emergency contraception in the United Kingdom alone.[10] They were in the business, just not willing to be in it in the United States.

Once it realized that large pharmaceutical companies weren't going to risk marketing EC in this country, the pro-choice movement looked to get into the pharmaceutical business itself. In 1997, Women's Capitol Corporation was created by leaders in the pro-choice movement with the exclusive purpose of marketing emergency contraception.

In 1998, the FDA approved the first emergency contraceptive product, and it was made available by prescription in one month. In the year 2000 alone, just two years after its formal introduction in the United States, EC prevented 51,000 abortions.[11] These were the results when just a few women, 2 percent, had used EC.[12]

Today, the potential for this abortion-prevention method has yet to be realized.[13] Less than 6 percent of all women report ever having used EC. Most of the American public, 60 percent, remain unaware that pregnancy prevention is still possible after unprotected sex.[14] (Compare this to Switzerland—a country with one of the lowest rates of abortion—where nearly 90 percent of sexually active young women and 75 percent of young men know about EC.)[15]

The barriers to timely access—and timely access is what matters with this drug—are considerable. Today, women have to get a prescription from their doctor, which means first getting an appointment. This alone can put a woman out of the effective time range, especially if it's needed on a weekend—and for most it is. (Then, as we've seen, some women who've landed a prescription run into pro-life pharmacists who refuse to dispense the medication.)

So, in April 2003, Women's Capitol Corporation took the next logical step. It submitted an application to the FDA to make Plan B available to consumers over the counter (OTC). Here, it seemed, was a way to prevent unwanted pregnancies and abortions. It wasn't dangerous. It should, Women's Capitol believed, be as available as any other medication.

In 2003, Women's Capitol Corporation was acquired by Barr

Pharmaceuticals.[16] (The acquisition would be completed in 2004, after Women's Capitol Corporation submitted its over-the-counter application to the FDA.) Apparently, the demonstration by Women's Capitol that EC could be marketed without incident cleared the way for a more established company to get into the field.

On December 16, 2003, a joint meeting of FDA advisory panels convened to review the Plan B application. FDA advisory panels usually have near-final say over crucial health questions. The Advisory Committee for Reproductive Health Drugs, one of those that met that day, is like all FDA advisory committees in this regard: it's supposed to be composed of impartial experts. The committee's job, at least until recently, has been to review the science and stay out of the politics. Are new contraceptive and abortion methods safe? Are they effective? What do the experts and the studies say? An advisory committee has traditionally seen its role as answering questions like these.

The year before, however, President Bush made several appointments that changed this emphasis. Perhaps Bush was uncomfortable relying on science, which didn't yield to his beliefs. Whatever the reason, he filled several vacancies on the Reproductive Health Drugs Committee with people more to his liking. He named several pro-life functionaries, people who, even though they were to rule on new contraception and abortion methods, oppose abortion and often birth control. Appointed to the committee were Dr. Joseph Sanford, a Utah physician who refuses to prescribe the birth control pill because he believes it is "incompatible with Christian values,"[17] and Dr. Susan Crockett, a board member of the American Association of Pro-Life Obstetricians and Gynecologists who cowrote an essay titled "Using Hormone Contraceptives Is a Decision Involving Science, Scripture, and Conscience."[18] But the key choice for the pro-life agenda would prove to be Dr. W. David Hager, who said that White House officials had been considering him as a candidate for surgeon general before selecting him to join the FDA panel. They chose him because, as he was told by White House officials, "there are some issues coming up we feel are very critical, and we want you to be on that advisory board."[19]

Though an obstetrician-gynecologist, Hager's expertise in his field was not widely recognized by his physician peers. Learning of Hager's appointment to the advisory panel, the chairman of the Ob/Gyn Department at the University of Kentucky Medical School, where Hager is a part-time professor, seemed surprised. "I was not aware of any credential that would single him out to do that,"[20] he said. Hager might list himself as a University of Kentucky professor on his résumé, but a university official clarified that, really, he had a slim and unprestigious connection. The spokesman told *Time* that Hager's appointment is part-time and voluntary and involves working with interns at Lexington's Central Baptist Hospital, not the university itself. Hager was "scantily credentialed," *Time* concluded.[21]

Of course, to pro-lifers, Hager seemed to have just the right qualifications. He might not be a top doctor or scientist, as were other advisory-panel members (including Dr. George Macones of the University of Pennsylvania, who had already authored more than 100 scientific articles,[22] and Dr. Charles Lockwood, chair of the Ob/Gyn Department at Yale University School of Medicine, who was also the past chair of the American College of Obstetricians and Gynecologists' Committee of Obstetric Practice and had more than 160 peer-reviewed publications).[23] Hager brought no résumé of peer-reviewed scientific works to this influential panel; instead, he brought a set of deep-felt beliefs. As he would later put it, "God has called me to stand in the gap. Not only for others, but regarding ethical and moral issues in our country."[24] An indication of where in that gap he stood can be gleaned from his publications. Hager's writings include a book titled *As Jesus Cared for Women: Restoring Women Then and Now*. Hager also cowrote with his then wife, Linda, *Stress and the Woman's Body*, which puts "an emphasis on the restorative power of Jesus Christ in one's life." The book not only recommends recourse to faith as a general salve but also pushes specific scripture readings and prayers for ailments like headaches and premenstrual syndrome.[25]

For the pro-life side, which was less concerned with scientific than with ideological credentials, Hager looked exemplary. Currently, he chairs the Physicians Resources Council at Focus on the Family.[26] He was also a spokesperson for the Christian Medical Association in its efforts to reverse the FDA's decision to approve medication abortion. And he advises both Concerned Women for America and the Medical Institute for Sexual Health—which leads the campaign against the condom. "He's really helped us with our credibility," explained Joe McIlhaney, the institute founder and anti-condom crusader whom Bush appointed to the Presidential Advisory Council on HIV/AIDS.[27] It might trouble his FDA panel colleagues that in his private practice, as *Time* reported, Hager refuses to prescribe contraceptives to unmarried women.[28] But to his pro-life supporters, it was no drawback at all.

At the December 16, 2003, meeting to consider making Plan B, the emergency contraception product, available over the counter, the FDA advisers heard expert testimony from the agency's own scientists as well as specialists in the field of contraception. They testified on the safety of Plan B and the appropriateness of removing the prescription requirement. During the day's proceedings, advisory-panel members asked questions of drug manufacturers and also heard from the public: forty-two individuals and groups weighed in. Of the forty-two that presented public testimony, twelve argued not to make EC more easily available. Of these, at least eleven were known emissaries of the pro-life cause. What no one in the day's proceedings publicly acknowledged was that each of those presenting testimony against EC didn't want only to stop it from becoming available over the counter. They hoped to ban it entirely.

The pro-life testimonials argued that easy access to EC would lead to widespread promiscuity, especially in the unmarried, a never-ending fear for the pro-life side. Not surprisingly, many who testified against EC seemed to think that no contraception had a place in American society. It's worth getting a feel for some of the day's arguments.

Jennifer Taylor of Human Life International argued against making EC available over the counter, explaining, "I am 30 years old and I've been married for two and a half years. I don't believe in contraception, and I don't use it, and I've never been pregnant, and my husband and I don't abstain as much as people might want to make you believe they do when it comes to NFP [natural family planning]." Taylor's argument seemed to be that since she didn't use contraception, then no one else should have the right to do so.[29]

Jill Stanek of Concerned Women for America, another pro-life group, argued against making the medication more widely available on the theory that it would somehow aid child molesters. "Making EC available would be a welcome tool for adult sexual predators who molest family members, children of friends or students," she told the FDA advisers. "They could keep a stash in their bedroom drawer or their pocket to give their victims after committing each rape."[30] (Of course, by this logic, you'd need to ban condoms as well, since predators could easily use one.)

Dr. William Colliton also gave testimony against EC, but he, like several others, did not reveal his pro-life credentials at the hearing (or that he opposes all forms of contraception). His past writings include "Birth Control Pill: Abortifacient and Contraceptive," in which he said, "There is an unarguable logic connecting the contraceptive act and the abortive act. They are both anti-life."[31]

Hanna Klaus, who runs an international abstinence-only group, also testified against EC. For her, contraception is a societal ill. In the past, she had managed to link contraception to black rage. In a 1997 essay titled "The Morning-After Pill: Another Step towards Depersonalization?" Klaus explained that she'd been overseas in the beginning of the sixties and returned to the United States shortly after the riots of the summer of 1968. She had a theory on the cause of that racial violence. "Until contraception became easily available, the black man could be told where he could live, where he could work, where he could be educated, but at least he could be a man; he could have children," she wrote. "With contraception, and five years later with abortion, anything a man could do could be made void by the woman. This may have been part of the driving anger of the summer of 1968."[32]

Right-to-lifers also told the FDA panel that EC, rather than stopping abortions, actually *is* an abortion. The science argued otherwise. According to the experts, the primary (if not the sole) method of action of emergency contraception is to prevent ovulation. In 2004, a meta-analysis of scientific literature conducted by experts at the Karolinska Institute in Stockholm found that the contraceptive effects of a one-time dose of levonorgestrel, the active ingredient in emergency contraceptive pills, "involve either blockade or delay of ovulation."[33] In the same year, researchers at the Chilean Institute for Reproductive Medicine found that emergency contraceptive pills interfered with ovulation 82 percent of the time.[34] Not coincidentally, EC is effective approximately 85 percent of the time if taken within seventy-two hours of unprotected sex.[35]

EC won't stop a sperm from fertilizing an egg. At least, as the scientists say, there is no evidence that EC works this way. Nor is there any evidence that if an egg has already been fertilized, EC will stop it from implanting in the womb and becoming a viable pregnancy.[36] Also, if a woman doesn't know she's pregnant and takes emergency contraception, it has no effect. The woman remains pregnant and studies show there's no harm to the fetus.[37]

But, as has become typical, when scientific evidence is against it, the pro-life side resorts to possibilities and doubts, however slim. Is it possible that in some rare cases EC inhibits implantation of a fertilized egg in the uterus? For the pro-life side, to stop a fertilized egg from implanting in the womb is to commit an abortion. The scientific community carefully responds that there is no evidence that this is what happens. Yet using the caution and restraint of scientists against them, pro-lifers act as if it has a "gotcha" moment. The fact that a responsible scientist can't absolutely *rule out* that as a third or fourth method of action there might be some slight inhibiting effect on implantation (which is what the responsible scientist says) is, for pro-lifers, tantamount to an admission that EC causes, by their standard, abortions. You see, the pro-life side says, the possibility can't be ruled out! It may be bad science, it may be bad faith. It doesn't matter. As Judie Brown of the American Life League told the FDA advisers, "The pills act to prevent pregnancy by aborting a child. For this reason alone the pill should not be available under any circumstance and certainly not over the counter."[38]

On the other side of the question, the backbone of the American medical establishment, including the American Medical Association, the American College of Obstetrics and Gynecology, and seventy other health and medical organizations, supported the application to the FDA to make EC available over the counter.[39]

As the day's proceedings unfolded, Dr. W. David Hager proved a key figure, perhaps the pivotal figure. Hager might be as ardently pro-life, pro-abstinence as any of the public witnesses, but from his perch on the advisory panel he framed his attack as apparent medical concerns. He wondered if EC would be abused by nine- and ten-year-old girls. "The plans for introduction of Plan B into the nontreatment setting need more evaluation if it is going to be generalizably available to a nine year old regardless, a ten year old regardless of, you know; there's no restriction," Hager explained.[40]

Other panel members seemed shocked by Hager's charge. "I would just like to make a point that it is extremely rare that the nine or ten year old has menstrual cycles," said panel member Dr. Abbey Berenson, a professor of pediatrics and ob-gyn at the University of Texas, "and so if we're going to talk about adolescents, let's talk about the mean age of menarche in this country is 12, and I can't imagine where a nine-year-old would get $40 to go buy Plan B over the counter and who would buy it for this nine year old."[41]

NO PLAN B   111

In fact, adolescents had been studied as part of the effort to determine whether EC was safe. Females from twelve to fifty had been sampled, including seventy-six between twelve and sixteen years old. Adolescents understood 60 to 97 percent of the drug-product package directions and materials, at a comprehension level similar to that of women as a whole and one that easily met standards previously accepted for the approval of other over-the-counter drugs.[42]

Hager objected to the sample size of twelve to sixteen year olds, which he contended was too small. In fact, adolescents represented 11.6 percent of the sample, nearly their proportion in the population of women of reproductive age, which is 12.6 percent.[43]

But for Hager the real bugaboo was that young child that he imagined abusing EC. Hager asserted:

> Well, I'm sorry, but there are young women that age [under twelve] who do start menstrual cycles, and although the numbers aren't large, it is enough of a concern that if there is an 11-year-old who is having a menstrual period and becomes sexually active, then she chooses to access this means of emergency contraception, and my only point is not the number. It's that we don't have information available on that younger age population.[44]

In weighing the pros and cons of wider availability of a medication that could prevent hundreds of thousands of abortions each year, Hager seemed stuck on an imagined nine or eleven year old who happened to have started her menses (less than 6 percent of girls younger than age eleven have started their menses)[45] and who was sexually active (4.2 percent of girls thirteen years of age and younger are sexually active),[46] and who knew that EC had been made over the counter, and who also had forty dollars to drop. For Hager, the lack of information on this tiny group—if it even existed—stood in the way of providing the 3 million women who face unintended pregnancies each year with a greater chance at prevention.

Some of Hager's fellow panel members seemed shocked. Not only did they think that the quality of Hager's argument was idiotic, but they suspected that he wasn't playing by the rules, the rules of science. As panel member Dr. Charles Lockwood explained, "Those who oppose OTC status for Plan B have taken a position that defies logic. Whether someone is pro-life or pro-choice, how can he or she oppose a measure that would reduce the need for abortions?"[47] Dr. Julie Johnson, an FDA adviser, explained of the EC over-the-counter proposal, "I've been on this committee, the Nonprescription Committee, for almost four years, and I would say this to be the safest product that we have seen brought before us."[48]

When the advisers voted on the safety of emergency contraception in an over-the-counter setting, there was unanimity. Even Hager voted that it was safe. And on the vote to make EC available over the counter, the advisers voted overwhelmingly in favor (twenty-three to four) of making EC over the counter. (Hager was among the dissenters.)

The FDA has in the past always based its decisions on the reports of its advisory panels. In an opinion piece in the *New England Journal of Medicine,* three physicians, including one panel member, explained, "Political considerations have wisely been kept out of the decision-making process. Although the FDA is frequently criticized by politicians and others for being either too lenient or too tough (depending on one's political or commercial perspective), the integrity of the process has seldom been questioned."[49]

This time, though, another unscientific process started almost as soon as the advisory panel finished its work. In response to the recommendation by the advisers, forty-nine pro-life members of Congress wrote to Bush urging White House involvement. The letter lobbied Bush to order the FDA to reject the company's application to make Plan B available over the counter. "We urge you and the Commissioner of the FDA to reject this recommendation of the joint advisory panels."[50]

Interestingly, members of Congress picked up on Hager's concerns. "We are very concerned that no data is available to suggest what impact this decision will have on the sexual behavior of adolescents and the subsequent impact on adolescent sexual health," the letter states.[51] The House members also reiterated pro-life concerns. Making Plan B available without a prescription could lead to more risky sexual behavior among adolescents and, they imagined, an increased incidence of STDs. Of course, the science suggested otherwise; studies have shown that when women do not require a prescription for EC, there is no rise in the rate of STDs.[52] Still, the intrepid members of Congress boldly concluded that easier access to EC "may ultimately result in significant increases in cancer, infertility and HIV/AIDS."

A month after receipt of the letter, FDA officials notified Barr Pharmaceuticals that the agency would extend its deadline for considering the switch to over-the-counter status. Sensing that politics had altered the process, three prominent physicians, including Alastair Wood, who served with Hager on the FDA advisory panel, published an article in the *New England Journal of Medicine* stating that "the recent decision by the FDA to postpone a decision . . . suggests that the FDA's decision-making process is being influenced by political considerations."[53] It outraged the three physicians. The FDA, which had for so long based its decisions on science, was now, they concluded, being guided by politics and faith. "Until now," the physicians wrote, "approval has been based on scientific evidence from well-designed clinical trials with adequate power to establish efficacy and rule out toxicity at some reasonable level of confidence." In a follow-up to their editorial, the authors explained that there was a proper place for politics. "If groups with moral objections wish to prevent the sale of a class of drugs, they should proceed through the legislative process," the physicians said. "They should not corrupt the scientific-review process of the FDA to achieve their ends. We believe that it will be very hard to put this genie back in the bottle. We squander public trust at our peril."[54]

Hager, along with fellow pro-life Bush appointees Crockett and Stanford, responded in a letter to the *New England Journal of Medicine*. They reiterated their concerns related to adolescent use. They also hypothesized a rise in STDs as a result of greater availability, a theory that seemed based on the idea that making EC over the counter would lead to an orgylike atmosphere. Hager and colleagues seemed prepared to do anything to make sex for pleasure difficult and unsafe. They also argued that the label should state that Plan B may act *after* fertilization. This last point was clearly a signal to pro-life fans that the issue was the pro-life definition of abortion. And it didn't even matter that Hager and Crockett had previously published work contradicting this argument. Writing along with twenty-two other pro-life ob-gyns, Hager and Crockett stated in 1998 that there is no evidence that hormonal contracep-

tion (and that's all Plan B is) prevents a fertilized egg from implanting in the womb.[55] Crockett had previously been even more explicit. She'd written in a separate article that "an extensive review of
pertinent scientific writing indicates that there is no credible evidence to validate a mechanism of pre-implantation abortion as a
part of the action of hormonal contraceptives."[56]

His previous statements notwithstanding, Hager felt moved to
write a "minority report" outlining his objections for the FDA commissioner, Dr. Mark McClellan (brother of White House press secretary Scott McClellan).[57] Hager said "someone" asked him to
write the report, though on different occasions he identified that
someone as different people. According to the *Washington Post*,
Hager said the request for the report came from "outside the
agency," contradicting his previous statements to two other journal-
ists in which he claimed that the request came from an FDA staff
member. An FDA spokeswoman said that the agency did not request that Hager write a report and that Hager sent what she called
a "private citizen letter" to Commissioner McClellan. "We don't
ask for minority reports and opinions," she said. "I've been advised
that nobody from the FDA asked him to write the letter."[58] Eventu-
ally, Hager coyly insisted, "I can't reveal" who told him to write the
letter.[59]

In May 2004, in an almost unprecedented move, the FDA decided against the recommendation of its advisers and its own scientists. Basing its decisions on the issues Hager and those pro-life
congressional members raised about adolescents, it declined to
make Plan B available over the counter. In the nonapproval letter to
Barr Pharmaceuticals to communicate his decision, Steve Galson,
acting director of the FDA's Center for Drug Evaluation and

Research, stated that the agency denied the over-the-counter status because studies had not been done on those fourteen years old and younger.[60]

If advisory panel members and medical experts had initially reacted to Hager as if insulted by his arguments, they now seemed infuriated—"hopping mad," said one.[61] Dr. Vivian Dickerson, then president of the American College of Obstetricians and Gynecologists, called the decision "morally repugnant."[62] It wasn't just the hijacking of a scientific process by fundamentalist politics, though that, certainly, was part of the anger. Dr. Charles Lockwood, panel member and chair of the Ob/Gyn Department at Yale University School of Medicine, wrote in an editorial, "We find it offensive that religious ideology and partisan politics have been introduced into the decision-making process regarding a public health issue."[63]

It seemed to further incense the physicians that the language of the rejection was couched in science when, to the physicians, the science was obviously on the side of Plan B. "The science and the law clearly support the switch to OTC status and that was reflected in the advisory committee's vote,"[64] explained panel member Dr. Alastair Wood, who had once been a Bush administration candidate to lead the FDA.[65] And the claims that youngsters would be at risk by greater EC availability were countered even by the experts in adolescent health. The American Academy of Pediatrics and the Society for Adolescent Medicine sent a letter to the Food and Drug Administration calling on the agency to reconsider its decision on Plan B. In a joint press statement the organizations stated:

We believe FDA reached an erroneous conclusion when it determined that there is not adequate data to safe use of Plan B by young women. There is adequate safety information about the use of emergency contraceptives both from Barr Research Inc.'s supplemental new drug application and data associated with long-term prescription use of these agents in the adolescent population.[66]

But to argue the science—indeed, to attempt to meet Hager's objections with evidence—was to fall into a trap. After all, if politics or faith is the issue, then science matters little. James Trussell, also a panel member and director of the Office of Population Research at Princeton University, explained, "The objection the FDA is offering in denying the switch to a non-prescription status is nothing more than a made-up reason intended to sound plausible. From a scientific standpoint, it is complete and utter nonsense."[67] Dr. Alastair Wood seemed almost saddened by this turn of events. "It's the first time I know of the [FDA] making a decision in which no one has produced any scientific basis for the decision," he said.[68]

Internally, the FDA staff was disgusted and disheartened. In an internal FDA memo obtained by the Associated Press, FDA commissioner Galson tried to quiet those feelings. Galson's memo said, "Some staff have expressed concern that this decision is based on non-medical implications of teen sexual behavior, or judgments about the propriety of this activity." Galson claimed that politics had not influenced his decision.[69]

Hager didn't credit politics either. He had another explanation. Six months after the FDA rejection, Hager gave a sermon at an Evangelical college. "I was asked to write a minority opinion that was sent to the commissioner of the FDA," he revealed to congregants. "I argued from a scientific perspective, and God took that information, and he used it through this minority report to influence the decision. Once again, what Satan meant for evil, God turned into good."[70]

In July 2004, Barr Pharmaceuticals tried to accommodate the FDA. It resubmitted its application, this time with an age restriction, allowing only those sixteen years or older to get EC over the counter. Teenagers would have to provide proof of age to buy EC, and those younger than sixteen would need a prescription for it. Under FDA regulations, the FDA had six months to review the application and make a decision. Six months later, in January 2005, the FDA invoked a rarely used "pocket veto," declining to issue a decision on the new application by the scheduled deadline.[71] The FDA, in its letter explaining the postponement to Barr, indicated that it is committed to completing its review of the application in the "near future." The FDA announced in July 2005 that it would consider the new application by September 1, 2005. On August 26, 2005, the FDA broke this agreement too—announcing it would not decide for another two months.[72] Upon this announcement, the FDA's director of the Office of Women's Health, Susan Wood, resigned in disgust. The administration announced she would be replaced by a veterinarian who had worked at the FDA for years. After women's groups balked at the appointment of a veterinarian to the position, the administration quickly revoked that appointment, denying it was ever made, though the vet had been introduced to agency staff as the new acting director of the Office of Women's Health and the agency's directory listed him under that new title as well.[73]

Scientists, doctors, and FDA staffers may have been disgusted by the agency's actions. However, Hager's victory, as well as his religious zeal, appealed to conservative groups such as the Family Research Council, Concerned Women for America, and the American Life League, who hailed the FDA decision.[74] Not that they were satisfied. Indeed, having won this battle in the face of vast scientific evidence, they seemed ready for more. As Judie Brown of the American Life League stated, "The best thing the FDA can do now for the American women and their progeny is to take the next logical step and remove these pills from the market altogether."[75]

chapter six

Pro-Lifers Abroad

DESPITE THE INTENSE CAMPAIGNS against contraception and reproductive rights in this country, American women are, comparatively speaking, blessed. To be pregnant in many other parts of the world is a dangerous undertaking. Women in the United States don't die during childbirth as 1 in 6 does in Afghanistan.[1] (The rate in the United States is 1 in 2,500.)[2] If you're a woman between fifteen and forty-five years old in the developing world, you're more likely to die from pregnancy than any other cause—imagine a life in which pregnancy is the leading cause of death! The difficulty is sometimes that pregnancies come too close together or else arrive too early or too late in life.[3] Women in the United States don't fear fistula; in fact, most don't even know what it is. But in sub-Saharan Africa, South Asia, and some Arab states, fistula is a common, and tragic, part of life. Caused by prolonged and obstructed labor and the unavailability of a C-section, a fistula is a hole that forms between a woman's vagina and her bladder and rectum. In most cases, the baby dies as a result of this kind of delivery. A woman who survives is left with a fistula, and lifelong incontinence. Urine and feces run down her legs. It affects more than 2 million girls and women worldwide.[4]

There are several strategies to prevent these kinds of horrible conditions. The availability of emergency surgery is one. But the most effective, and most feasible, remedy is simpler. It's been known for a long time that family planning saves mothers' lives. Whatever convictions you cherish, the facts are clear: as contraception use rises in a country, maternal, fetal, and infant deaths decline. As Save the Children reports in *State of the World's Mothers 2004*, "Increased access to and use of modern contraception can lead to dramatic improvements in infant and maternal survival rates."[5] In Finland, one country in which contraception is inculcated in the culture, 75 percent of women use birth control. In Finland, the lifetime risk of a mother dying in childbirth is 1 in 8,200, and 4 out of 1,000 Finnish infants do not make it to their first birthday. Compare this to Niger where 4 percent of women use birth control. In that African country, 1 in 7 mothers dies in childbirth, and 156 of 1,000 infants die before reaching age one.[6]

In reality, one of the most pro-life things to do is give people the means to plan their pregnancies. The world community knows this, and since, for many years, the international debate on reproductive health has taken place beyond the reach of fevered American ideologues, health leaders have been able to enact policies that save lives. The prevailing theory among most nations today, except the most religious (like Iran's mullahs and our pro-life groups), is that family planning is critical. This is true not only to save mothers' and infants' lives but also, as international groups recognize, to try to reverse the cycle of poverty that devastates whole societies. As economist Jeffrey Sachs, whom *Time* named one of the world's one hundred most influential people in 2005,[7] explains in his book *The End of Poverty*, "One reason for the poverty trap is a demographic trap." The demographic trap occurs when impoverished families have a lot of children. "When impoverished families have large numbers of children, the families cannot afford to invest in nutrition, health, and education of each child," explains Sachs. "They might only afford the education of one child, and may send only one son to school. High fertility rates in one generation, therefore, tend to lead to impoverishment of the children and to high fertility rates in the following generation as well. Rapid population growth also puts enormous stresses on farm sizes and environmental resources, thereby exacerbating the poverty." (And, in the contemporary world, Sachs notes, poverty is a breeding ground for terror.)[8]

Although there is widespread agreement among health experts and many economists that a cure for many of the world's ills is voluntary family planning, there is a growing and powerful enemy against making that cure available. The U.S. pro-life movement's campaigns against contraception aren't limited to our national borders. With the exception of the Vatican, every single international campaign against contraception is based in the United States, promulgated by groups whose belief in the sanctity of life actually keeps others from saving their lives. It is our pro-lifers who are leading the movement to deprive women in the world's most desperate regions of contraception. Recently, they've been very successful.

Why would the pro-life movement undertake a campaign against life-saving practices? And how is it that they accomplish this goal around the world? The story of how one small pro-life organization in Virginia unleashed a vicious, and damaging, attack on a vital branch of the United Nations not only illuminates the thinking of the pro-life movement but also illustrates its political muscle within the Bush administration, muscle that extends across the globe.

Though the conservative allies of pro-lifers rail against the United Nations for political reasons, the UN is, in large part, not a political organization. It is a relief agency. It provides assistance in the most dangerous and unstable places on earth. The role of one of its agencies, UNFPA,* includes a laundry list of life-saving interventions in the reproductive field: delivering babies, creating healthy births, ensuring that women are well enough to become mothers again, and giving families the methods to space children. UNFPA also spearheads the global campaign to end fistula.[9] It works in more than 126 countries, most of which are poor and risk getting poorer since they have the highest rates of population growth. Often, UNFPA works in war-torn settings, dispensing emergency contraception to women who have been raped during military conflicts (an increasingly common act of war) and ensuring that pregnant women can deliver babies safely when they are driven into refugee camps.

UNFPA does not provide abortions. In fact, "UNFPA . . . does not provide support for abortion services," the group says explicitly. "We work to prevent abortion through family planning, and to help countries provide services for women suffering from the complications of unsafe abortion."[10] Instead of abortions, UNFPA provides about 41 percent of the world's total needed contraceptive services.[11] It does all this on a meager budget of $500 million, supplied by countries that believe in its work. The world's poorest countries give what they can. (In 2004, Rwanda gave $500, Afghanistan $100, Guatemala $1,568, Turkmenistan $1,662.) For the most part, UNFPA relies on the contributions of wealthier nations—the Netherlands ($72 million), Sweden ($35 million), Norway ($33 million), Denmark ($30 million), Japan ($39 million), and

*The United Nations Population Fund uses the acronym UNFPA based on its former name, the United Nations Fund for Population Assistance.

the United Kingdom (34 million).[12] Until recently, the United States was among the wealthy nations that donate the lion's share of UNFPA's budget. Its 2002 promised contribution of $34 million represented 13 percent of the agency's budget at the time.[13]

UNFPA is by many standards a model of what the UN does well. It has a tremendous impact on the poorest people, and it does so on a shoestring. As Sachs, speaking at an event in 2003, explained, "UNFPA's work is absolutely vital. I'm not getting into the culture wars issues. I'm speaking as an economist."[14]

UNFPA became a "vital" organization after 1994, the year it organized the International Conference on Population and Development in Cairo. One hundred and seventy-nine UN member nations signed on to a "program of action," representing a crucial shift for the agency and unwittingly setting it on a collision course with the American pro-life movement. The program of action argued, in essence, that women are the drivers, the change agents, who can improve the lives of families and nations. As such, "the empowerment of women and improvement of their status are important ends in themselves and are essential for the achievement of sustainable development,"[15] UNFPA concluded. The keys steps to empower women include education and skill development, as well as family planning. "The [program] advocates making family planning universally available by 2015, or sooner, as part of a broadened approach to reproductive health and rights."[16]

UNFPA declined to get into the abortion business and didn't consider it a method of family planning. It did state, "In circumstances in which abortion is not against the law, such abortion should be safe. In all cases, women should have access to quality services for the management of complications arising from abortion. Post-abortion counseling, education and family planning services should be offered promptly, which will also help to avoid repeat abortions."[17]

Importantly, the Cairo meeting shifted the focus from specific "demographic targets" (numeric goals in population growth) to giving couples the ability to plan the size of and to space their families. This was a fundamental change, and seemed to be written with one nation in mind: China.

Since the early seventies, China, in an effort to curb soaring population growth—China has one-fifth of the world's 6.6 billion people on just 7 percent of the world's arable land[18]—has employed extremely aggressive policies. In 1979, it dictated one child only for many families and forced abortions or sterilization on many women who violated the mandate. There have been reports of "above-quota" newborns being killed by doctors under pressure from local officials.[19] Other brutal enforcement tactics include destroying the homes of women or their relatives when they violate the one-child rule. Today, the Chinese claim to no longer force abortions or sterilizations, but they do impose a "social compensation fee" for those who have more than one child, and the fines can be as high as eight times the average Chinese yearly salary.

Many international groups opposed forced abortions and sterilizations, but UNFPA was the first international agency to publicly say that even China's "social compensation fee"[20] was wrong. After years of discussions, UNFPA, the only international agency working on these issues in China, managed to convince the government in Beijing that there is a better way to control population explosion. The agency hoped to show China that giving people the right to choose their family's size would be effective in stabilizing population growth. In 1998, the Chinese government agreed to a test. It would end its one-child policies in 32 counties (out of 2,500). The UNFPA approach was voluntary birth control. After five years, the results looked promising. The new direction helped rein in the population explosion; the number of women giving birth remained the same, and at the same rate. Also, the abortion rate in the 32 counties fell from 24 percent of all pregnancies to 10 percent, a rate lower than that of the United States.[21] The Chinese government, impressed with the results, paid to expand the program to 800 more counties.[22]

It was hard to argue with these results. Even the United States seemed to recognize the good work of UNFPA. In 2001, Secretary of State Colin Powell stated that UNFPA did "invaluable work through its programs in maternal and child health care, voluntary family planning, screening for reproductive tract cancers, breast feeding promotion, and HIV/AIDS prevention."[23] All seemed to be rosy. Good work, promising outcomes. In the aftermath of the invasion of Afghanistan, the Bush administration turned to UNFPA. Afghani maternity wards were in rubble. Women fleeing that conflict were delivering babies on the sides of dirt roads. The Bush administration gave UNFPA $600,000[24] to reestablish maternity wards and lower the skyrocketing maternal death rates.[25]

Just a few months later, however, something happened. The Bush camp did an about-face. Initially, President Bush had requested $25 million for UNFPA for 2002. Congress raised the contribution by $9 million, to a total of $34 million. Then, suddenly, the Bush administration announced that the White House planned to freeze *all* U.S. funding of UNFPA.

The impetus? The White House had heard from Congressman Chris Smith, chair of the Pro-Life Caucus in Congress. A tiny pro-life group based in Virginia had contacted Smith. For years, the group, the Population Research Institute (PRI), had been running smear campaigns against UNFPA. Recently, PRI issued a report claiming that UNFPA was helping implement the coercive one-child policy in China—even though its sole mission in China was to end these policies. Congressman Smith, apparently with no investigation, partnered with PRI, offering the fringe group the imprimatur of Congress. (He invited the group to testify at a congressional hearing, and sent a letter to the president on its behalf.)

By freezing the funding, President Bush made the United States the only donor country to deny funding to UNFPA for non-budgetary reasons.[26] His reason, he said, was the Kemp-Kasten Amendment to the 1985 foreign-aid bill (officially, the Foreign Operations, Export Financing, and Related Programs Appropriations Act), which prohibits giving foreign-aid money to any organization that, as determined by the president, "supports or participates in the management of a program of coercive abortion or involuntary sterilization."[27]

PRI had been at its campaign for years. Finally, though, the political climate turned favorable. PRI has just six staffers—yet aligning itself with its pro-life brethren, and a pro-life president, it wielded enormous political power. This tiny group reversed elements of U.S. foreign policy.

PRI began as a program of Human Life International (HLI), a Catholic pro-life organization that "fight[s] the evils of abortion, contraception, sex education," the usual pro-life suspects, among others. ("In some countries, HLI is the pro-life movement," it claims.)[28] In 1996, PRI incorporated as an independent organization "to enable it to operate more effectively in the secular world."[29]

Also, Human Life International continues to provide the "over-whelming majority" of PRI's funding. Plus, HLI's founder, Father Paul Marx, remains deeply involved in PRI and serves as chairman of its board.[30] PRI, like its former parent, and like so much of the pro-life movement, opposes every form of birth control (except natural family planning and abstinence). As its Web site explains, the agenda of PRI is "common to all truly pro-life organizations," and it includes being "against artificial contraception."[31] PRI likes to say that one of its missions is to "end human rights abuses committed in the name of family planning." One specific PRI goal is to prevent international relief agencies from providing voluntary contraceptive services, which it considers a human rights abuse. It appears it will go to considerable lengths to prevent what it considers abuses.

In 2001, PRI sent a paralegal, Josephine Guy, to China for four days to "investigate" UNFPA in Sihui County, one of the thirty-two in which the Chinese government agreed to end its one-child mandate. Guy had never been to China and doesn't speak Chinese. Still, with the help of an interpreter, she seemed to get along well with the Chinese. "We struck up casual conversations, and asked people if they would talk to us about family life," she explained in "Full Report of UNFPA's Involvement in China." "People were friendly and pleased to have visitors from outside of China. As the conversation began in earnest, more and more people would invariably gather around, curious to discover the reason of our visit. Many times they would chime into conversations. At times it was difficult to carry on conversations, so many people were talking at once."[32]

Through these casual conversations, Guy apparently became convinced that UNFPA was complicit in the Chinese government's coercive one-child policy. Guy said that women in Sihui County told her the one-child policy was still in effect. Guy and her inter-preter met with one doctor and four women who said, according to Guy, that "voluntarism does not exist within the county's family planning program." One of these women was at the doctor's office to receive an abortion, accompanied by several friends. Her friends "asserted that their friend wanted to continue her pregnancy, but the law forbids it," Guy reported.[33]

The most damning evidence against UNFPA, according to Guy, was not the one-child policy, which, after all, UNFPA also opposed. It was Guy's allegation that despite its stated opposition to forced abortions, UNFPA was somehow complicit in them. Guy didn't spell out how UNFPA aided and abetted the Chinese government. But she did claim to have discovered an empty desk at the Chinese Office of Family Planning in Sihui. Guy said she was told by an un-named worker that the desk belonged to UNFPA. The empty desk, Guy added meaningfully, "in fact touches the desk of a Chinese family planning worker." To Guy, this desk was evidence that UNFPA was turning its back on long-standing policy, and working hand in hand with the Chinese to force women to have abortions.

Upon Guy's return, pro-life leaders in the U.S. House of Repre-sentatives Henry Hyde (R-IL) and Christopher Smith (R-NJ) orga-nized a congressional hearing at which PRI could present its "evidence." The October 2001 hearing seemed to reach its conclu-sion even before beginning, as indicated by its title, "Coercive Pop-ulation Control in China: New Evidence of Forced Abortion and Forced Sterilization."[34]

Five days after the hearing, at the request of UNFPA, an indepen-dent investigative team was sent to China to look into PRI's allega-tions. The team was organized by UNFPA and tapped distinguished

participants. The four-member team included Dr. Nicolaas Biegman, the Netherlands' former ambassador to the UN and NATO;
Noemi Ruth Espinoza, the deputy ambassador of Honduras to the
United Nations; Jana Simonova, minister counselor of the Czech
Mission to the United Nations; and Emolemo Morake, first secretary of the Botswana Mission to the United Nations. Biegman explained their goal this way: "The mission I led had a single goal: to
see if we could uncover any credible evidence that the UNFPA violated the human rights of Chinese citizens or was complicit in any
way in helping the Chinese Government violate the human rights
of its citizens."[35] Before his team's trip to China, Biegman contacted PRI in order to gather as much information regarding their
allegations as possible. "Unfortunately, they were either unwilling
or unable to provide a response," he stated.[36]

Four months later, in February 2002, Dr. Biegman told the Senate Foreign Relations Committee:

> I would like to state for the record that I accepted this invitation with
> an open mind. Although I am familiar with UNFPA and believe that
> its work has, on balance, been very helpful in the developing world,
> everyone who works on these types of issues understands that the
> possibility for abuse exists and must be vigilantly guarded against. I
> traveled to China prepared to uncover and weigh the facts impar-
> tially and to respond fairly and accurately to whatever I might find.[37]

The team's investigation in China lasted five days. They visited a
total of seven family-planning clinics, service centers, and hospitals
in the county from which the allegations stemmed and also in another county that receives UNFPA funding. And they, like PRI,

interviewed Chinese citizens "on the street, in family planning and mother and child health clinics, in villages—using two independent interpreters and without any Chinese government officials present. Our random interviews with people on the street included over three hours of discussions."[38]

The impartial team came to different conclusions than PRI had. Indeed, they couldn't have been more different. In conversations with Chinese citizens, "No one expressed any grievances or complaints or knew of any abuses in recent years," Biegman's team reported. "Such abuses had occurred in the past, they said, but not in the present."[39]

Biegman also investigated the desk that had been so important to the PRI allegations. "The desk that supposedly comprised the UNFPA office in Sihui County that was constantly referred to in the testimony before the House Committee simply does not exist," Biegman's team concluded. "That purported UNFPA office, which formed a central part of the testimony of PRI is a complete and utter fabrication. UNFPA has no offices in China outside Beijing."[40] Biegman and his team of independent investigators found "absolutely no evidence that the UNFPA supports coercive family planning practices in China or violates the human rights of Chinese people in any way."[41]

In fact, Biegman and fellow investigators discovered just the opposite.

Our investigation found that UNFPA's program . . . is helping to show Chinese officials that voluntary family planning programs are the best way to reduce population growth. The overall impression that the team came away with was that the Chinese approach had changed in the two project counties we visited. It was also apparent that the UNFPA does not support the Chinese Government's one-child policy in name or practice and does not take any part in supporting or managing the Government's program.[42]

Not satisfied with the report of this investigative team, the State Department decided to organize its own. In May 2002, the State Department sent a three-person delegation to China. The delegation included a former ambassador to Israel and Thailand; a former career foreign services officer who worked in Ethiopia and Nicaragua as well as the State Department, White House, and U.S. Mission to the United Nations; and a public health professor from the University of Arizona.[43]

The delegation spent fourteen days in China and visited five of the thirty-two counties in which UNFPA works. Upon return, the team sent a "report of the China UNFPA Independent Assessment Team" to Secretary of State Colin Powell. In it the team explained,

> During our visits to five of the 32 counties we asked many SFPC [State Family Planning Commission of China] officials, doctors of the local hospitals under the Ministry of Health, county administrative officials, and ordinary Chinese in spontaneous/no-notice encounters on the street, in a school, or in factories whether they were aware of any recent coercive abortions or involuntary sterilizations. All answered in the negative although some admitted that prior to the joint SFPC/UNFPA program there had been such cases.

The U.S. State Department team also failed to discover any desk or UNFPA staff members in Sihui County.[44]

The U.S. delegation concluded, "We find no evidence that UNFPA has knowingly supported or participated in the management of a program of coercive abortion or involuntary sterilization in China." And so, like the international delegation, it recommended that the United States release the $34 million in funding to UNFPA.[45]

In April 2002, the British also sent over yet another investigative team, this one composed of three members of Parliament (MPs). The British delegation was led by a pro-life member of Parliament, Edward Leigh. "The MPs were able to select the houses and the women that they wanted to speak with at random in the villages," their report noted.[46] "No one expressed any grievances or complaints of any kind, or knew of any abuses, in the years when UNFPA had supported family planning in the villages." Their unimpeded investigation also found no evidence of coercion in the areas where UNFPA operates. "On the contrary, there was evidence UNFPA is trying to persuade China away from the program of strict targets and assessments," British pro-life MP Leigh told the *Washington Times*. "My personal line is British or U.S. funds should not be used for coercive family planning, and I found no evidence of such practices in China."[47] The British team seemed to come away enthusiastic. "The delegation was convinced that the UNFPA programme is a force for good, in moving China away from abuses such as forced family planning, sterilisation and abortions," the MPs observed. Indeed, even the pro-life head of the delegation joined in endorsing UNFPA work. "It is vitally important that the UNFPA remains actively involved in China, with continued financial support from the UK and other Western Governments," the MPs' report concluded.[48]

Has any program ever been more thoroughly investigated than UNFPA in China? Former director of UNFPA's Information and

External Relations Stirling Scruggs says a total of 145 diplomats have visited the Chinese counties where UNFPA operates. "It's the most-reviewed development project in the world," Scruggs says, explaining that no one raised concerns about what they saw.[49]

Nonetheless, American pro-life groups were undeterred. Indeed, the complete vindication of UNFPA time after time, the glowing reports even by some pro-lifers, seemed to make the American pro-lifers only more determined. Who needed evidence? They demanded action. On June 20, 2002, Concerned Women for America, the Family Research Council, Feminists for Life, Focus on the Family, Christian Coalition, Abstinence Clearinghouse, American Life League, Connecticut Right to Life, Pro-Life Maryland, Staten Island Right to Life, Right to Life of Central California, Missouri Right to Life, Alabama Citizens for Life, Rhode Island State Right to Life, Illinois Right to Life, as well as Human Life International, PRI, and more than 100 other pro-life groups sent a letter to President Bush.[50] Despite the fact that not one shred of independent evidence had been uncovered to support the allegations of PRI's paralegal, the pro-life groups had clearly gotten their marching orders. They professed to still have "grave concerns about the State Department investigation," not to mention the British and the international investigations. They claimed the State Department's investigation and the others were "international whitewashes." The Bush administration had temporarily frozen funds for UNFPA. In 2002, the pro-life groups implored Bush to deny UNFPA its congressionally approved funding once and for all.[51]

The month after receiving the pro-life coalition letter, the Bush administration ignored its own investigation and changed the status of the UNFPA funds. Jay Lefkowitz, White House deputy assistant to the president for domestic policy, known as the point person for Christian conservatives in the White House,[52] was a "key player" in drafting a memo that explained the policy options. "[White House spokesman Scott McClellan] declined to explain why an official [Lefkowitz] charged with setting policy within the United States would be involved in a decision about a program that operates abroad,"[53] *Knight Ridder* reported. But from the memo itself, one reason was clear. The administration wanted to understand the politics, the *domestic* politics, of the decision. How would Senate Democrats and abortion opponents react? The memo made the answers clear, according to the *Washington Post*.[54] And so the funds, once frozen, were now canceled by the Bush administration in 2002.

In a poignant (and perhaps belligerent) touch, Bush left it to Secretary of State Powell to deliver the bad news. Powell, a longtime UNFPA supporter, favored continuing the funding.[55] Indeed, he fought to get UNFPA at least some of the money.[56] "Powell really got sandbagged on this one," an unnamed official explained to Agence France-Presse.[57] In a Salon.com article titled "A $34 Million 'Political Payoff,'" journalist Michelle Goldberg explained that the announcement "seemed especially humiliating for Colin Powell, who had to defend a decision that contradicts the recommendation of his own staff and everything he himself has ever said about the Population Fund."[58]

Global reaction to the defunding was swift. UN ambassadors from more than fifty African nations wrote to Secretary Powell asking him to restore the funding and expressing their confusion at how the United States could take an action that so disproportionately affects Africa. They wrote, "The least developed countries, 34 of which are in Africa, receive the bulk of UNFPA's funding and will be most affected."[59] They were particularly worried that the decision could harm family-planning efforts as well as programs to combat HIV/AIDS.

The decision to cancel funding to UNFPA would have been sad enough if the pro-life campaign had ended there. It didn't. The Bush administration, ever intent on winning pro-life votes, went after friends and colleagues of UNFPA, defunding them, or threatening to, if they collaborated with UNFPA. It was guilt by association. (And the guilt wasn't even really guilt. Don't forget that no one but a handful of pro-life enthusiasts believed that UNFPA did anything but excellent work.) In 2004, the Bush administration held an "informal" meeting with UNICEF. The United States would no longer provide financial support to the agency's joint programming because of concerns that funds for UNICEF and UNFPA could not be kept separate.[60] The United States likewise stopped funding Marie Stopes International, a British charity, and its work on AIDS prevention for Asian and African refugees. The reason? It worked with UNFPA.[61] The State Department offered to continue to fund six organizations that work with Marie Stopes International on AIDS prevention on one condition. They had to stop working with Marie Stopes. The six organizations refused the State Department's offer, turning their backs on American money. They stated that they would not cease their joint work over "baseless allegations."[62] The administration abruptly cut off funds for a Global Health Council conference, taking back one-third of the conference's funding just weeks before it was to take place. Why? Because the executive director of UNFPA, Dr. Thoraya Obaid, was scheduled to speak on ending child marriage.[63] As Stirling Scruggs, a former director of UNFPA, explained, "It reminds me of the McCarthy era. We're blackballed. They've defunded us, and even that isn't enough. It's unbelievable."[64]

The funding cut had several effects. In the near term, loss of American money forced UNFPA to end or curtail some programs, including several that ensured safe childbirth in Kenya and in Bangladesh (where one in forty-two women dies during pregnancy or delivery).[65] In Algeria, a program to train midwives was cut back.[66] In Nepal, which has one of the highest rates of maternal death in the world, efforts that had reduced maternal and child deaths were not able to grow to meet the demand. In Vietnam, a program to train 4,000 healthcare workers working in remote villages in prenatal care could not expand. In Central Asia, where the spread of HIV/AIDS is mounting, UNFPA's HIV/AIDS prevention efforts, along with family planning, emergency obstetric care, and modernization of hospital equipment, were unable to grow.[67] In Uganda, where 506 out of 100,000 pregnant women die each year, UNFPA provides communication devices to women facing pregnancy complications so they can call to be taken to health centers if an emergency emerges. That project, called the Rescuer Program, was also scaled back as a result of the U.S. funding cut.

There were more diabolical effects. Stripping $34 million from UNFPA, the world's largest provider of contraceptives, translated into deaths. According to one calculation, the loss of the $34 million adds 4,700 maternal deaths and 77,000 infant and child deaths each year to the world's toll of suffering. It also results in about 800,000 abortions each year, most illegal and unsafe.[68] This isn't an isolated or politicized calculation. Indeed, it's at the lower end. A 2002 report from the Johns Hopkins School of Public Health cites estimates that each $1 million decline in contraceptive assistance results in 360,000 additional unintended pregnancies, 150,000 more induced abortions, 11,000 more infant deaths, and 800 more maternal deaths.[69] Using these estimates to calculate the casualties of the pro-life campaign, you end up with at least 12 million unintended pregnancies, 5 million abortions, 374,000 infant deaths, and 27,000 maternal deaths. That's every year.

There was one salutary effect, this one from other donor nations. At first, they seemed baffled by the U.S. decision. Then they seemed almost sad, as if a favorite relative had been stricken with mental illness. "The decision of the USA is entirely incomprehensible," said German development minister Heidemarie Wieczorek-Zeul. But confusion and sadness soon turned to anger. "In reaching its decision, the American government has contravened all international obligations to enable women to gain access to family planning services,"[70] added Wieczorek-Zeul.

If the Bush administration intended to coerce the world community into following its lead, the gambit failed. Indeed, to the consternation of pro-lifers, the Bush administration's heavy-handed policy has had just the opposite effect. In response to U.S. withdrawal of funding, other countries have pledged to increase their contributions. Poul Nielson, the European commissioner of development and humanitarian aid, called on other nations to fill in what he called "the decency gap."[71] Ireland said it would double its support to UNFPA to $2.5 million annually.[72] Canada gave an additional $4 million to UNFPA.[73] The European Union raised its contribution by 32 million euros to be used over three and a half years.[74]

The Bush administration, now with an extra $34 million on its hands, decided to route the funds to another government agency, the U.S. Agency for International Development, sometimes called

USAID. Perhaps the Bush administration (and especially its Powell wing) imagined this as a way to support the UNFPA work without the political hostilities. After all, as part of its mandate, the development agency helps provide basic contraceptive care in impoverished nations—though in half as many as UNFPA does. (Like UNFPA, the U.S. development agency does not provide or fund abortion services.)

Pro-lifers, though, weren't happy with the move. The always-candid American Life League president, Judie Brown, summarized the pro-life position in a press release titled, "Redirection of $34 million from UNFPA to USAID a 'Stab in the Back.'" Brown complained that what President Bush "has given to pro-lifers with one hand, he has taken away with the other." It was clear what Bush had given. But what had he taken away? To Brown and her allies, the stab in the back was that Bush had turned around and given the money to, as Brown put it, the U.S. Agency for International Development's "abortifacient 'contraceptives' program."[75]

Clearly, PRI came away from its encounter on the world stage emboldened. It had mastered the tactic of the false allegation, the allegation that, once lodged, everyone must respond to. It used this tactic in other venues. In Kosovo, PRI claimed that UNFPA conspired with Slobodan Milošević to "engage in ethnic cleansing by reducing Kosovars' high birth rate" and in "genocide" against the Muslims. PRI seemed happy to stoke the ethnic hostilities with false and incendiary claims that appeared to have one purpose: to intimidate UNFPA workers. Representatives of PRI, along with another anti-family-planning, pro-life group, C-Fam, went to Kosovo hospitals and asked staff not to work with UNFPA.[76] The trouble for the pro-lifers was that UNFPA had provided emergency contra-

ception to female refugees in Kosovo who had been raped and
wanted to prevent pregnancy—this apparently was the basis of the
"genocide" charge. "The morning-after pill which has been available in Europe for over 20 years is simply an elevated dose of normal birth control pills. It prevents a pregnancy from beginning but
it can not interrupt an established pregnancy. Therefore it is not an
abortifacient," explained UNFPA spokeswoman Corrie Shanahan,
"To suggest that a woman who has lost her home and members of
her family and then been subjected to rape . . . should be denied
access to a product which is legal and available in her country . . . is
absurd."[77]

In Afghanistan, PRI again claimed UNFPA introduced "genocide," this time in Afghan refugee camps. PRI seemed to have fallen
in love with the "genocide charge." Why not? The immunity it enjoyed courtesy of its powerful Washington backers allowed it to say
just about anything. PRI went on to claim that UNFPA had sent
"abortion kits" to Afghanistan. The PRI accusations were picked
up by the Vatican newswire Fides, which then got picked up by the
French news service Agence France-Presse, giving them an air of
credibility.[78] The facts were otherwise, not that facts slowed PRI.
Afghanistan's Ministry of Health requested UNFPA's assistance as
"an urgent priority for national reconstruction." UNFPA opened a
mobile hospital in Kabul to offer emergency obstetric care to save
the lives of women and babies during delivery. The mobile hospital
was set up while a damaged maternity hospital was being rebuilt
with UNFPA support.[79] The supplies PRI referred to were labor
kits essential for safe birthing for home deliveries, including rubber
sheets, soap, gloves for assisting the birth, and clean razor blades
for cutting umbilical cords.[80]

Reaching yet higher rhetorical heights, PRI claimed that UNFPA aid workers were planning "abortion jihad" in Iraq after the fall of Saddam Hussein. By now, it was clear that something else was stirring the PRI pot. The jihad charges—indeed all of PRI's charges—were absurd on their face. The abortion charges had always been a cover. What really bothered PRI (and most of its pro-life colleagues) wasn't that UNFPA was doing awful things in China or in Bosnia or Afghanistan or Iraq. What dismayed the pro-lifers is deeper and broader and, for the rest of us, scarier. What really unsettled PRI, and so many pro-lifers, was the effort to make contraception widely available and with it the social benefits of planned families. They didn't like that money was going to contraceptives, which was, after all, the true purpose of most UNFPA programs. It was no doubt easier to rally forces against "coercive abortions" or "abortion jihad," no matter how spurious the charge. But their true concerns were elsewhere. As the Web site of PRI bluntly states, "Family planning is inherently coercive in a developing country context."[81] To these avid pro-lifers, contraception is just as bad as the abortion it might prevent. Indeed, this is the reasoning that runs through the confounding opposition of the pro-life movement to so many programs that might further the goals it holds dear. The Pill, the IUD, the condom, they were all the same devilish trick. USAID, UNFPA, it didn't matter. A contraceptor is a contraceptor is a contraceptor and always to be opposed. As the Reverend Thomas J. Euteneuer, president of Human Life International (PRI's parent organization), explains, "Remove birth control from the equation and . . . [w]omen will begin to love motherhood again and not feel guilty about loving motherhood. . . . Nature would rule marital and human relationships again and not technology."[82]

There was something further. It seemed clear that what heated up PRI's emotions, and the emotions of so many pro-life groups, was where contraception might lead. They feared that women, availing themselves of family planning, might participate as equals in society. The real worry was that these women would become independent and ambitious, thinking and acting for themselves. PRI wasn't really against UNFPA, at least not for the reasons it stated. Maybe it didn't even believe its own charges against the agency—few others did. Really, PRI wanted UNFPA and *every* contraceptor kept at bay. In China with its mammoth population, the stakes were huge. But the fall of Iraq and the vast new possibilities it represented had recently brought PRI fears to the surface. "If we Americans behave in Iraq as we behave in other countries, upon Baghdad's surrender we will fly in teams of population controllers and 'gender advisors,'" writes PRI president Mosher. "They will inaugurate programs which will subject Iraqi children, especially girls, to graphic sex education programs. They will stock Iraqi medical clinics with condoms and contraceptives." Ignore for a moment how like the Islamic mullahs Mosher sounds. Consider the fear that he expresses. It isn't even about contraception. It's more basic. It's the notion of empowering Iraqi women or Chinese women or any women. Mosher continues, "It gets worse. The 'gender advisors' (this is what they are really called), will provide assertiveness training to Iraqi women, urging them out of the home into the marketplace. They will organize special courses (reserved for women, of course) in which they are urged to run for public office and start their own businesses."[83] Clearly, for staunch pro-lifers like Mosher, the fear of women holding public office or starting their own businesses or, one suspects, disobeying their husbands is the soil in which opposition to abortion and contraception and sex education takes root.

What is most alarming is that these fears, so antiwoman (and antimodern), find safe harbor in the pro-life movement and, now, in the Bush administration. A wave of pro-life extremists—remember that PRI has only a handful of staffers—now seems to have undue influence on key elements of U.S. policy. Perhaps that's what so shocks the rest of the world. Nicolaas Biegman, the former ambassador who investigated PRI's claims against UNFPA in China, asserts, "It's not really understood by the rest of the world how a superpower like America can be influenced in such a deadly way by four or five fanatics," adding, "It's amazing."[84]

chapter seven

A World without *Roe*

INTERNATIONALLY, THE PRO-LIFE MOVEMENT seems to do whatever it wants. At home, what stands between us and the pro-life way is one key court decision, *Roe v. Wade.* The day after *Roe* falls, federal protections of the right to abortion will disappear. With that will come threats not only to abortion but also to many kinds of birth control. The moment *Roe* goes, state laws will step into the breach. For years, pro-life legislators have been quietly crafting state laws with just such a day in mind. (Since Bush took office, there have been nearly 2,000 pro-life restrictions and proposals considered in the states, and approximately 150 have been enacted, including 29 in 2004 alone.)[1] Without much public attention, these legislators have created a different kind of world, one that will remain dormant until the day *Roe v. Wade* goes away.

One result is that the day after *Roe* is overturned, the right to abortion will be threatened, if not quickly made illegal, in no fewer than twenty-one states* (Alabama, Arkansas, Colorado, Delaware, Ken-

---

*Interestingly, the pro-life movement contests this statistic. It has its own figures. Abortion, it says, would be instantly outlawed in only seven states. Why the disparity? Their answers are revealing. Partly, it's because the pro-life movement refuses to consider abortion illegal if a state permits abortion even to save a woman's health. If a doctor is allowed

tucky, Louisiana, Michigan, Mississippi, Missouri, Nebraska, North Carolina, North Dakota, Ohio, Oklahoma, Rhode Island, South Carolina, South Dakota, Texas, Utah, Virginia, and Wisconsin; the Territory of Guam appears likely to ban abortion too).[2] To put these figures in perspective, in 2000, approximately 400,000 women from these states had abortions.[3] In another twenty states, abortion is likely to remain legal, at least in the near term. (These states are Alaska, California, Connecticut, Florida, Hawaii, Maine, Maryland, Massachusetts, Minnesota, Montana, Nevada, New Jersey, New Mexico, New York, Oregon, Tennessee, Vermont, Washington, West Virginia, and Wyoming.)[4] In the remaining nine states (Arizona, Georgia, Idaho, Illinois, Indiana, Iowa, Kansas, New Hampshire, and Pennsylvania, along with the Commonwealth of Puerto Rico and the District of Columbia),[5] abortion rights will be uncertain. Three of these states (Arizona, Idaho, and Indiana) would probably quickly ban abortion since both legislative houses and governors are currently pro-life.[6] In most of the remaining six, uncertainty may act the same as a ban. In only two of these states today are the attorneys general solidly pro-choice. Thus, doctors who perform abortions in these up-for-grabs states won't be sure if they're protected by the law. And, in the absence of clarity, a politically am-

---

to perform an abortion to rescue a woman whose pregnancy is compromising, say, a vital organ, then, to the pro-lifers, abortion is "still legal" in that state—even though the vast majority of women in those states couldn't legally obtain an abortion. The pro-lifers also don't factor in an assessment of the political leanings of the states' legislatures or governors on the abortion issue. Pro-choice advocates took such factors into consideration. They gauged a state's likelihood to enact new bans or revive old ones. "New Study Reveals That Overturning *Roe* Will Not Impact Legality of Abortion in Most States," Life Legal Defense Fund, press release, June 28, 2005. http://www.overruleroe.com/Press/press_release_06-28-05_print.htm (accessed July 1, 2005).

bitious prosecutor could accuse doctors of violating the law—even charge them with murder—and throw them into lengthy, costly, and perilous court battles.[7] The result is that effectively, if not definitively, abortion will likely be lost as a right in thirty states if *Roe* falls.

The practical implications of more than half the states either outlawing or no longer defending one of the country's most common surgical procedures are significant. These days there are just 1,800 doctors providing abortions to more than 1.3 million women each year.[8] (Between 1982 and 2000, there was a 37 percent decline in the number of abortion providers in the United States.)[9] A third of those doctors, 600, reside in states in which abortion would no longer be clearly legal.[10] They would, with little doubt, stop providing abortions. Women who need abortions will rush into the states where it remains legal, but now they will have many fewer doctors able to serve them.

If *Roe* is overturned, it's likely that a clandestine, illegal underground will emerge again to meet the need for abortions, a need that virtually no one believes will disappear. After all, research shows that even when abortion was previously illegal in the United States, women had abortions. Indeed, the number of women who had abortions has remained fairly constant over the decades. The only thing that legality changes is whether abortions will be safe. That, at least, was the critical difference the last time abortion was criminalized. In her important book, *When Abortion Was a Crime*, Leslie Reagan documents the ten decades of U.S. history when abortion was outlawed. According to Reagan, the lack of established institutions to provide abortions forced many women to do it themselves. She writes, "The increased difficulty of locating an abortionist and the skyrocketing prices for abortion surely contributed to the numbers of women who attempted to self-induce their abortions." Word of solutions was passed along informal and often unreliable networks. Introducing bleach was one all-too-common and often fatal method tried by women. Reagan cites the cases in Chicago in the 1950s in which young women had been "injected with lye" to induce abortions. "One woman described taking ergotrate, then castor oil, then squatting in scalding hot water, then drinking Everclear alcohol," writes Reagan. "When these methods failed, she hammered at her stomach with a meat pulverizer before going to an illegal abortionist."[11] Before *Roe*, some women tried to induce abortions with whatever they could find, including the infamous coat hanger.

The situation was most desperate for the poor. Indeed, the young and the low income have been the biggest victims of the outlawing of abortion. Women of means inevitably travel to states (or countries) in which abortion is legal. But the vast majority of women seeking abortion care in the United States today are poor. Indeed, two-thirds of all women seeking abortion report it's because they cannot afford to have a child.[12] Fifty-seven percent of the women receiving abortions in the United States have incomes below 200 percent of the poverty line (that's less than $28,000 for a family of three).[13] These, clearly, are the people most likely to resort to other means.

If the United States rolls back *Roe*, then it seems clear abortion will fall to less experienced, perhaps greedy, and certainly secretive hands, exactly how it once was. "A woman who went to Tampa for an abortion in 1963 recalled being examined by the doctor, then being put in a van with several other women, the entire group blindfolded, and then driven to an unknown location where the abortions were performed," writes Reagan. One woman recalled her fear when she took a friend to the illegal abortionist whom she had previously visited herself: "As I handed her over to strangers at the outside door of the apartment building where the abortion was to be performed, then met the mysterious contact in the park who carefully counted the money, and then waited, waited and waited, I realized how totally at the mercy of unknowns and unknowables my friend was, and I had been."[14]

Of course, in an illegal environment, the other problem is not with abortions, but with aftercare. "A Detroit student who found she was pregnant in the spring of 1968 went with a friend to an abortionist who 'was upstairs over a store. We were both scared to *death*. The man did the abortion and said not to call him if I had problems.'"[15] For a doctor to say, "Don't call me in the case of a complication" sounds particularly heartless. But when abortion was illegal, caring for a patient who suffered after a clandestine abortion was dangerous for physicians too. A doctor could be held as an accessory to a crime. Doctors were pitted against their patients, and the implications were far-ranging. Even miscarriages were suspect. Was a miscarriage perhaps really an illegal abortion? A lot of physicians just didn't want to have anything to do with providing care even *after* an abortion because of the risk of prosecution. A woman might have induced her own abortion, and shown up on a doctor's doorstep hemorrhaging and near death. If she died, the doctor could be in trouble. "Police arrested physicians simply because they were the last physician attending the patient and they had not made their report to the coroner," says Reagan.[16]

In our current climate, in which refusal to provide medical services is becoming more common (remember, pharmacists can refuse to fill prescriptions for even birth control), it's easy to imagine that physicians could refuse care for women who are miscarrying either naturally or unnaturally.

If *Roe* were reversed and abortion became a crime, the situation that doctors face could very well be worse than the last time it was illegal. Before the 1970s, those who performed illegal abortions were typically prosecuted only if the woman died. And even if she died, few of those cases (in one state, less than 25 percent) resulted in prosecution.[17] In the future, however, the danger could very well be broader. Those performing criminal abortions could be tried not for injury to the consenting woman, but for murder of the fetus. A raft of new pro-life laws, passed since *Roe,* protects the fetus from injury. Thirty-four states have passed Unborn Victims of Violence legislation and fetal-protection laws. In many states, these laws apply to the earliest stages of pregnancy, and in some even before a pregnancy is established.

In some states, the legislation frighteningly protects not only a fetus but even a fertilized egg, even before it implants in the womb, the transition that makes it a pregnancy. According to the National Conference of State Legislatures, "At least 15 states have fetal homicide laws that apply to the earliest stages of pregnancy ('any state of gestation,' 'conception,' 'fertilization' or 'post-fertilization')."[18] The real problem with this legislation is that there's no way of knowing whether an egg has been fertilized until it implants in the womb. While abortion remains legal, doctors and women are mostly shielded from these statutes. If *Roe* goes, it's anyone's guess how laws protecting fertilized eggs would be applied.* A compas-

---

*According to National Right to Life, Pennsylvania's law applies to the "unborn child" and "fetus," which is defined as "an individual organism of the species Homo sapiens from fertilization until live birth." Texas applies its statute to "an unborn child at every stage of gestation from fertilization until birth." Mississippi, Oklahoma, and Kentucky apply the moment of "conception," a term that is vague in the law and has often been inter-

sionate physician could face murder charges, including life in prison and possibly the death penalty. As the ACLU explains, "Zealous anti-choice prosecutors may try to intimidate abortion providers by threatening to use the statutes as grounds to indict them for murder."[19]

Anyone contemplating a post-*Roe* world should bear in mind that most of us haven't experienced anything like it. Almost the entire current population of women of childbearing age has grown up with a legal right to abortion. A woman who was fifteen in 1973 would now be at the end of her fertile years. The *Roe* decision was the beginning of a fundamental societal shift. Indeed, it is, by now, part of our idea of what we're entitled to as Americans. The greatest evidence of this is that most Americans believe *Roe* should remain intact. A Gallup poll taken in July 2005 found that 65 percent of Americans think *Roe* should stay the law of the land—this statistic is all the more stunning when we learn that the same poll found that only 51 percent of Americans consider themselves pro-choice.[20] Thus, a significant portion of people who personally oppose abortion—about one-third—apparently recognize that there should be ways of discouraging abortion other than an outright ban.

Clearly, though, the will of the people is secondary when it comes to abortion. One thing that both pro-life and pro-choice advocates agree on—and there isn't much—is that *Roe* is almost over. The latest blow is the announced retirement of Justice Sandra Day

preted to mean fertilization. The statutes in Arizona, Illinois, Missouri, Nebraska, North Dakota, Ohio, South Dakota, Vermont, and Wisconsin apply to "any stage of prenatal development." "State Homicide Laws That Recognize Unborn Victims (Fetal Homicide)," National Right to Life. http://www.nrlc.org/Unborn_Victims/statehomicidelaws092302.html (accessed October 20, 2005).

O'Connor. Some say that O'Connor was the vote that allowed *Roe* to survive, weakened but intact. In previous challenges, O'Connor, the first woman Supreme Court justice, wrote that any restrictions on the right to choose cannot pose an "undue burden" on a woman's access to legal abortion, language that stymied several attempts to restrict abortions.

Similar cases will be decided with the help of her pro-life successor. Already, President Bush has signaled his preference for pro-life justices. He nominated John Roberts to replace Chief Justice William Rehnquist, who passed away in September 2005. Roberts has not openly acknowledged his pro-life politics. Perhaps he will follow the path of Justice David H. Souter, who was also appointed by a pro-life president but whose decisions on the Court have helped protect *Roe*. But that seems unlikely. The fact that the most extreme pro-life groups rushed to endorse his nomination is a pretty good sign that pro-choice people have reason for concern. Operation Rescue, a group best known for blockading abortion clinics,* gloats:

> Already, the rabid pro-abort leaders are *screeching in horror* at the thought that John Roberts might be a strong pro-lifer. . . . They know that Roberts was the lawyer for the Justice Department who won the famous "Title X" case that cut off federal funding of abortions. They know that his wife Jane is a strong pro-life activist who

---

*As a principal deputy solicitor general for the U.S. Justice Department, Roberts co-authored a government brief arguing Operation Rescue was immune from any lawsuits sought under federal civil rights law stemming from the organization's blockades of abortion clinics. "Roberts' Record as Government Lawyer, Private Attorney, Judge," Associated Press, July 20, 2005.

has worked for many years with 'Feminists for Life' and other organizations. And they know that John Roberts went to bat for Operation Rescue back in 1992—in a case before the Supreme Court known as Bray et al. v. Alexandria Women's Health Clinic et al.

He also stated in a previous case that, "*Roe* was wrongly decided and should be overruled."[21]

Still, Roberts's confirmation should not change the vote on *Roe* since he replaces a pro-life justice. The majority on the Court in favor of abortion rights will remain either six justices to three, or five to four, depending on the case. In the rosiest view, even if O'Connor is replaced with a pro-life judge, that still leaves a slim one-vote majority in favor of *Roe*. The resignation of one more pro-choice justice would almost certainly leave *Roe* unprotected. Currently, as every Court watcher knows, the strongest supporter of abortion rights on the Court, according to Naral Pro-Choice America, is Justice John Paul Stevens.[22] He is also, at eighty-five, the oldest justice. How many eighty-five year olds work in your office? (Lately, pro-lifers have been directed to pray for the retirement or death of a pro-*Roe* justice like Stevens.)

And, make no mistake, Bush may claim that he has no litmus test on abortion for his nominees. Yet he has a long record of nominating judges who are opposed to a woman's right to legal abortion. Nearly all fifty-two of Bush's nominees to the federal appeals courts are hostile to the concept of the right to privacy, on which the *Roe v. Wade* decision was built, and fifteen of them have extreme pro-life records.[23]

Some pro-life activists believe cases that could overturn *Roe* are already in the pipeline. Pro-life senator John Cornyn (R-TX), a member of the powerful Judiciary Committee, told the *Washington Times* that *Roe v. Wade* will face a direct challenge in the upcoming Supreme Court term. "Whether *Roe v. Wade* should be overturned is not only an issue likely to come before the court . . . it is already before the court," he said.[24]

Of course, exactly how a hostile Court would reverse *Roe* isn't clear. It could take the most extreme position and grant the fetus (and the embryo) the status of a person. This would theoretically make it murder to perform an abortion as early as the moment of implantation. However, what appears more likely is that the Court will attack the theory on which *Roe* is based. In 1973 the Supreme Court found that abortion is constitutional because it concluded that privacy is a guaranteed right that protects, among other things, a woman's right to make private decisions about her body, including the decision to have an abortion. The right to privacy is, however, not explicitly listed in the Constitution, unlike free speech or free assembly. In *Roe v. Wade*, however, the majority found that bodily privacy is an implied right. A new Court could determine that nothing in the Constitution, explicitly or implicitly, guarantees this general right to privacy. Or it might agree with abortion opponent Chief Justice William Rehnquist who wrote in his dissent to *Roe*, "I have difficulty in concluding, as the Court does, that the right of 'privacy' is involved in this case."[25] Either way, *Roe v. Wade* would seem to be doomed.

If the Court decided that abortion is no longer a constitutional right, then not only would state legislative bodies fill the vacuum. The Senate and House both consist of pro-life majorities. Congress could move to ban abortion across the country. Congress has already rehearsed a similar action. In 2003, Congress enacted and

President Bush signed the Federal Abortion Ban, criminalizing abortions as early as twelve weeks—currently it's legal through the twenty-fourth week. Because *Roe* is intact, appellate courts have found that Congress's attempt to halve the time frame for some legal abortions violates the Constitution. If, however, *Roe* were overturned, the outcome would no doubt be different.

With *Roe* still the prevailing law of the land, we see inroads being made into important protections, and we have hints of some of the consequences. Already, for example, we glimpse how zealous prosecutors use available laws to punish anyone they can get their hands on. In some cases, prosecutors behave as if *Roe* is already gone. Consider the 2005 case of seventeen-year-old Texan Erica Basoria. She had asked about an abortion at a visit to her ob-gyn but was told, falsely, it would turn out, that she could not get an abortion.[26] (In effect it was true. She was more than sixteen weeks pregnant at the time, and as a result of pro-life pressures there are practically no abortion providers in Texas who perform procedures at this stage in a pregnancy, even though it is legal.) Feeling she had no other recourse, she asked her boyfriend to help her. Her nineteen-year-old boyfriend, Geraldo Flores, did as she asked, and stood on her stomach. She miscarried. The prosecutor saw a crime. Since abortion is still legal, Erica was not charged. But under Texas's version of the Unborn Victims of Violence Act, the prosecutor went after her boyfriend, who was convicted of homicide and sentenced to life in prison.

Just a year earlier, in 2004, a teenage couple from Michigan tried to get an abortion. They were too frightened to tell her parents, so they called a crisis pregnancy center. Predictably, they were given false information about her rights. (They were told by the crisis pregnancy center there was no way to avoid involving her parents.)[27] Believing they had no other options, the girl asked her boyfriend to strike her in the belly with a twenty-two-inch, souvenir-size baseball bat, which he did over the course of several weeks. The girl miscarried. Their actions were discovered, the *Detroit News* reported, "when the girl talked about the series of events that led to the miscarriage while at a high school leadership conference. . . . The adult facilitator of the conference contacted the Michigan State Police."[28] The sixteen-year-old boyfriend was tried for intentionally causing harm to a fetus, a felony.[29] The girl's father rallied to the boy's cause. "This is a very tragic situation," he explained. "Two very good children thought the one thing they couldn't come to us with was this pregnancy. It is a shame and this prosecution is a sham."[30] The boy's lawyer pinned the blame on the labyrinth of pro-life laws leading them to their decision: "These kids were totally desperate," the lawyer said on Fox News. "They tried a number of desperate methods to create a miscarriage. They got incorrect advice from official hotlines about the law and about the medical consequences of a safe legal abortion. These kids didn't have access to smart, compassionate sex ed. . . . They didn't feel they could go to their parents. They completely panicked."[31] The teenage boy, because he was a juvenile, faced imprisonment until age twenty-one. (If he were an adult, he would have faced fifteen years in prison.) In September 2005, the court gave the boy probation and ordered that he do community service. The judge sent him to work at a pro-life crisis pregnancy center, the same type of center that gave him and his girlfriend the inaccurate information that led them to take matters into their own hands. His father protested the nature of the community service sentence, stating, "This is an in-your-face [move] by the judge. Why not send him to Planned Parenthood, where he could see all sides of being a parent?"[32]

His girlfriend was not charged because Michigan's fetal-protection law currently does not apply to an action taken by the woman on herself. However, that soon might change. The legislator who authored the law under which the boy was charged explained in January 2005, "When I wrote it, nobody contemplated the mother cooperatively participating in the beating of herself to kill the unborn child. We'd simply change the law and under those circumstances the mother would be chargeable."[33] He later added, "This will be one of the first things we do in the next session. What we're going to do is remove any immunity that a woman in this case may have."[34]

Clearly, pro-life states are eager to prosecute women. In some instances, they have already found ways. In 2005 in South Carolina, Gabriela Flores, a twenty-two-year-old migrant farmworker from Mexico, discovered she was pregnant. Gabriela already has three children. She speaks no English and has a fifth-grade education. When the man who got her pregnant refused to take responsibility, she believed her only choice was an abortion. She didn't have access to a doctor; the funds would have been difficult to come by. So, instead, she had a friend from Mexico send her Cytotec, a commonly used ulcer medication that can also cause a miscarriage. (This is the method most doctors believe American women will resort to if abortion is outlawed and they take matters into their own hands.)

Flores's action was discovered when she told someone who told someone else who called the police. Flores wrote a handwritten statement in Spanish to the police: "I knew that I was not going to be able to support four kids—two here and two in Mexico. Please understand me. They need me a lot. They are little. Please forgive me." Flores did not report the matter, or go the hospital, she said, because another woman had told her if she did she would be thrown in jail. Flores explained to the police, "I was very afraid for my kids because they were going to be left alone."[35]

Prosecutors considered charging Flores with murder, but didn't because they could not prove the fetus would have been viable. Instead, she recently spent four months in jail for violating a little-known state statute against performing an abortion on herself. Prosecutors then, apparently convinced she hadn't suffered enough, charged her with the separate crime of "unlawful abortion" as well as failure to report the abortion to the county coroner. If convicted, she may spend two more years in state prison, and be forced to pay a $1,000 fine.[36]

That these convictions occur now, with *Roe v. Wade* intact, is an ominous sign. As a lawyer for the boy in the Michigan case pointed out, "What this case represents is a harbinger of things to come." After all, *Roe* now protects most people most of the time. With *Roe* gone, the number of acts of desperation by women and girls will multiply, as will convictions. And since pro-life compassion seems to extend only to the unborn—indeed, for those making difficult decisions they revel in the harshest penalties—we may one day see women condemned to death for abortion.

Imagine a country without *Roe* in which more than 1 million women a year—the number who currently get abortions—would have to consider whether they, too, might end up charged with a crime like Gabriela Flores.

Of course, some on the pro-choice side warn that the real damage could be done even without overturning *Roe*. *Roe* could stand, just gutted. Add enough pernicious restrictions, and the Court could, in effect, do away with *Roe* while still keeping it on the books. Already, we see this happening state by state. Clinic staff in many states are required by legislation to read pro-life scripts, complete with medical inaccuracies and scare tactics, to their patients before caring for them. (Interestingly, those doctors and clinic staff aren't granted, unlike pharmacists handed prescriptions for birth control, the right to refuse.) In some state legislatures, pro-life laws are being floated that require all abortions after twelve weeks be performed in hospitals, all the while knowing that in those states no hospitals offer such care. By now the overwhelming majority of states won't permit Medicaid to pay for an abortion. Even in states where Medicaid isn't allowed to pay for abortion, Medicaid *is* often required to pay for abortions in the case of rape, incest, or to save the woman's life. Yet most women and girls can't get their state Medicaid office to comply with that law. Teenagers in many states must often navigate the courts to seek a judicial bypass if they want to get an abortion without their parents' involvement (that's true even if a parent is responsible for the pregnancy), though they can continue their pregnancy (which poses a risk fifteen times greater to their health and life than an abortion does) without any parental involvement at all.

For teenagers, the situation may get increasingly dire even with *Roe* still intact. The U.S. House of Representatives recently passed the Child Interstate Abortion Notification Act (CIANA), and the Senate is expected to pass it by the end of 2006.[37] This legislation requires teenage girls to carry the laws of their state with them. Of course, most pregnant girls already involve their parents in a decision as crucial as whether to have a baby or not. Even in states that don't require parental involvement, 61 percent of parents knew of their daughter's pregnancy. The problem is with families that function poorly, or don't function at all. Among minors who didn't tell a parent of their abortions, 30 percent had either experienced violence in their family or feared being forced to leave home.[38] Before CIANA a worried girl could travel to a neighboring state to avoid arduous parental-consent laws. Under CIANA, that will no longer be true. More girls who had good reason not to tell their parents of their plans will most likely be forced to involve a parent in the decision.

And the situation could get much worse. In 2005, for example, the Supreme Court will hear the case *Ayotte v. Planned Parenthood of Northern New England,* a case about a New Hampshire parental-consent law that offers no exception if the girl's health is in danger. Planned Parenthood explains, "The law would have forced physicians to wait to provide emergency medical care until the young woman was facing imminent death."[39] But just as important as the specific issue in this case is the fact that the Court will review the basis on which it determines whether *any* restriction on abortion is constitutional. Justice O'Connor famously wrote that a law can't place "an undue burden" on any individual woman who wants an abortion. What if that standard were changed? What if a law no longer had to unduly burden any individual woman seeking an abortion to be unconstitutional but instead had to unduly burden *every* woman the law applies to seeking an abortion to be unconstitutional? This is the new standard the government proposes in *Ayotte.*

A post-*Roe* world will have more dire surprises in store. The implications are far-ranging and not just for women seeking abortion. Without *Roe,* an infertile couple's chance to use in-vitro fertility technology (IVF) may be severely limited. In IVF, many fertilized eggs are implanted in a woman's womb. But by implanting more than one, the hope is that the odds will be greater that one or two will "take," resulting in a pregnancy. Often, though, more than one or two fertilized eggs, sometimes even five, implant. All multiple pregnancies are considered high risk because of the increased likelihood a woman, and the fetuses, will suffer from dangerous ailments, some potentially fatal. For instance, the fetuses in multiple pregnancies have an increased risk of birth defects and genetic disorders. The more numerous the pregnancy, the more likely are these risks. Often, fertility specialists counsel couples to "reduce" the pregnancy to ensure the healthy survival of the other embryos and the woman. This procedure is called "selective reduction," which really is a gentle way of saying an abortion. In a post-*Roe* scenario, the states that ban abortion will also ban selective reduction. Thus, women trying desperately to have a child may have to accept three or four or five.

The effect of *Roe*'s disappearance on people who opt for tests to determine birth defects will also be profound. Amniocentesis and diagnostic ultrasound are standard procedures on pregnant women thirty-five and older that can reveal the gravest fetal anomalies, like, for instance, anencephaly. In anencephaly (also known as "no brain" syndrome),[40] there is no forebrain or cerebellum. Given such a terrible condition—or any other of the serious defects that make life outside a womb impossible—most women choose to end a pregnancy. Without *Roe*, that won't be possible. The recent experience of a military couple foreshadows this brave new post-*Roe* world. Their fetus was diagnosed with anencephaly, and they asked for the military health plan to cover the $3,000 cost for an abortion.

The federal health plan refused, citing the Hyde Amendment, which prohibits the use of federal funds for abortion. The couple challenged the case in court. The Justice Department took up the case against the couple and prevailed. The court ruled against the couple, stating, "Abortions performed for suspected or confirmed fetal abnormality . . . do not fall within the exceptions permitted within this language of the statute and are not authorized for payment."[41] In this decision, the court ruled the termination of a pregnancy due to grave defects is purely elective (and, therefore, it follows, would be banned if abortion were outlawed).

Yet all these realities of a world without *Roe* are not even the most insidious. The unheralded (and diabolical) implication of overturning *Roe* is that it begins a chain of events that calls into question the right to contraception, an outcome that no doubt enthuses many pro-life advocates. Though it seems difficult to remember now, contraception was not always legal. As late as 1965, the state of Connecticut criminalized the use of contraception. In *Griswold v. Connecticut,* the Supreme Court struck down the Connecticut law. Their reasoning would prove crucial not only in *Griswold* but also as the basis for the Court's finding in *Roe.* Justice William O. Douglas, drafting the opinion of the Court on *Griswold,* famously wrote: "Specific guarantees in the Bill of Rights have penumbras formed by emanations from those guarantees that help give them life and substance." He found these penumbras and emanations in "various guarantees" that, as put forth in the First, Third, Fourth, Fifth, and Ninth Amendments to the Constitution, "create zones of privacy."[42] It was these zones of privacy that allowed the Court to find, in the case of *Roe v. Wade,* as in the case of *Griswold,* that abortion was, like contraception, a constitutionally guaranteed right. The reasoning from *Griswold* to *Roe* was straightforward: if a woman had the right to make the private decision to forestall a pregnancy, then she could also by the same right decide to terminate a pregnancy.

If the Court reverses *Roe* by determining that this right to privacy is not guaranteed by the Constitution, and that is the bet of most legal scholars, then what happens to the right to contraception, which rested on the same right? If you poison the roots, you kill the tree. Several justices on the Supreme Court already openly disdain the constitutional right to privacy. Antonin Scalia and Clarence Thomas are among them. Thomas offers a direct quote of Justice Potter Stewart's dissent in *Griswold* as his own opinion, writing, "I 'can find [neither in the Bill of Rights nor any other part of the Constitution a] general right to privacy.'"[43] In fact, Thomas lately considers the *Griswold* decision so baseless he no longer wastes his breath deriding it. Instead, he has hung a sign in his Supreme Court chambers that reads, "Please don't emanate in the penumbras."[44] Justice Scalia shares Thomas's view. As "Courting Disaster 2005," a report by People for the American Way, explains:

> Scalia's and Thomas' views are so extreme that their rulings would also do widespread damage by reaching beyond the specific issue of abortion. . . . They contend that the Constitution does not protect any right to privacy concerning reproductive or bodily integrity whatsoever. If this view comes to command a majority on the Supreme Court, it would threaten landmark decisions like the 1965 ruling in *Griswold v. Connecticut,* and could permit state laws banning the sale or use of contraceptives or similar steps to violate privacy rights long taken for granted by all Americans.[45]

To People for the American Way president Ralph Neas, the clear movement away from the notion that people have a constitutionally protected right to privacy is scary. Indeed, most right-wingers would find it scary as well—except, perhaps, when they are looking to impose their morality on others. "Most Americans would find it unthinkable that their state government could make it illegal for married couples to use contraceptives," says Neas. "But the unthinkable could be at hand if the radical right has its way with the American courts. *Griswold* and other decisions protecting Americans' privacy rights could be overturned if the Supreme Court is filled with justices who don't believe the Constitution protects individuals from the prying eyes of government, even in our bedrooms."[46]

Griswold, and the right to privacy on which it was built, already has many outspoken pro-life critics—the Family Research Council and Concerned Women for America are among those that seem to hope for a world in which the right to privacy disappears, and the government can impose its views on how and why people should enjoy sex.[47] (Homosexuals, it's worth noting, have been protected by the same privacy guarantees.) Pro-life senator Rick Santorum explained the right-wing view to the Associated Press: "This right to privacy that doesn't exist in my opinion in the United States Constitution, this right that was created, it was created in *Griswold.*"[48]

Most Americans might believe they understand the difference between contraception and abortion, between preventing a pregnancy and terminating one. The most active pro-lifers, as should be clear by now, don't. They don't really distinguish between birth control and abortion. And, frighteningly, they've latched on to a legal argument that could obliterate that distinction in the eyes of the

Supreme Court. For the religious Right, the destruction of privacy is like hitting the trifecta: it could abolish abortion, contraception, and important gay rights. If the foundation for *Griswold* were to be found untenable, then hold on to your hats. The right to use contraception could well become a state-by-state matter too.

A close look reveals that the groundwork is already being laid for the day when that federally protected right to contraception fades away. Science may define pregnancy as beginning at the moment it can be discovered, implantation. But state laws crafted by pro-lifers neatly circumvent science. Currently, eighteen states have enacted provisions that define pregnancy as beginning at fertilization or conception.[49] There is no scientific or medical evidence that birth control pills (or any form of hormonal contraception) prevent fertilization. But a lack of evidence may not be enough. Indeed, it seems likely that the next target of the pro-life forces will be contraception.

Rarely examined passages in state legal codes are just the stepping-stones the pro-life movement needs to challenge the legality of contraceptives. When states define pregnancy as beginning at some unknowable moment—the moment of "conception," as five states put it—they place sexually active women in a precarious position. The fact that a powerful political movement that abhors sex outside of marriage or even inside marriage when not for baby making has amassed legal weapons to use not just against abortion but against contraception can't be coincidental. Nor is it heartening that only a "penumbra" in the law has shielded us all from the religiously motivated and their desire to police our most intimate of activities.

For the engaged pro-lifer, attacks on abortion are really just a stage-setter, preparing for a more sweeping pro-life drama: the abolition of contraception, and, more broadly, the creation of a society in which the only acceptable reason for sex is procreation.

As I write this, Harriet Miers has just withdrawn her nomination to the Supreme Court and Samuel Alito has been nominated instead to replace Justice O'Connor, long the court's swing vote on matters related to abortion. Yet the debacle of Miers's nomination was revealing. As the process built steam, pro-life groups debated, cavalierly and publicly, whether Miers was very likely or very, very likely to vote to overturn *Roe v. Wade.* Some Senators even suggested that pro-life leaders asked for guarantees from top White House aides, including king-maker Karl Rove. Following a private conversation with Rove, one pro-life leader said: "When you know some of the things that I know, that I probably shouldn't know, you will understand why I have said . . . that I believe Harriet Miers will be a good justice."[50] To pro-choicers, Miers's thoughts on *Roe* were not the most frightening thing about her. After all, she appeared unwilling to be pinned down on an even more sweeping right, the constitutional right to use contraception as decided in *Griswold.* Miers's view seemed to fluctuate depending on who put the issue to her. She gave the Republican Chairman of the judiciary committee the impression that she respects *Griswold* and the right to privacy it established. But when the pro-choice Chairman happily reported this, she hastened to correct him: that's not what she meant to say at all.[51] Privacy apparently is in play, just as the pro-life forces wish.

As much as she tried to hint she would heel to the agenda of pro-life fundamentalists, in the end, they served as the architects of her withdrawal. There were too many unanswered questions, she did not "feel" pro-life enough. It may have not mattered how arduously she tried to prove herself to pro-lifers. Their source of doubt may have rested on another set of factors: she is a childless, ambitious, life-long single, working woman. That biography, as much as any views she held, didn't fit with the pro-life outlook, and it no doubt made her seem untrustworthy.

Samuel Alito brings the intellectual heft and judicial experience expected of Supreme Court nominees, another drawback to Miers, who had no judicial experience. His resume also suggests a more acceptable paternalistic view of the family. His decisions as an appeals court judge, for example, included one that required a pregnant woman to notify her husband before she could get an abortion. (Alito's judicial views seem to rest firmly on his traditional concept of marriage.[52]) Justice O'Connor pointed out flaws in his viewpoint when the Supreme Court struck down that decision. The same reasoning would follow, O'Connor argued, that "pregnant wives should notify their husbands before drinking alcohol or smoking. Perhaps married women should notify their husbands before using contraceptives or before undergoing any type of surgery that may have complications affecting the husband's interest in his wife's reproductive organs . . . Women do not lose their constitutionally protected liberty when they marry."[53] For pro-choicers, the larger worry is that Alito seems decidedly pro-life, and not just on the details. The instant and unified support for Alito's nomination among the pro-life ranks should make one thing clear: They have no doubt he will vote to overturn *Roe*.

And so here we are. *Roe v. Wade* is teetering and may be about to topple. If that day comes will the pro-lifers pack up and retire? The evidence suggests otherwise. The outlawing of abortion will likely be followed by another intense campaign, much of it already under-way, this one against contraception. Those well-worn "Stop abortion now" pro-life banners may not even require alteration since, conveniently, the pro-lifers want us to believe that contraception is abortion. Science, reason, fact and social reality may not be sturdy enough to withstand the force of a politically powerful and infinitely pious movement of those who believe that by governing the most intimate parts of our lives they are doing God's work. The question is: will the American people stand up to a few energized crusaders hellbent on imposing their views on how we all ought to live?

Notes

Preface

1. Dan Barron, "A Land Still Divided on Abortion," letter to the editor, *New York Times,* January 23, 2003.

Chapter One

1. "Pharmacists Who Won't Dispense Morning-After Pill Fired," Associated Press, February 12, 2004.

2. Liz Austin, "Denial of Emergency Contraception for Texas Woman Raises Moral, Legal Questions," Associated Press, February 24, 2004.

3. Gretel C. Kovach, "Pharmacist Refuses to Refill Birth Control: North Texas Woman Denied Pill Because of Moral Conflict," *Dallas Morning News*, March 31, 2004.

4. Diana Washington Valdez, "Fabens Pharmacist Won't Fill Orders for Birth Control Pills," *El Paso Times*, August 10, 2004.

5. "Laconia Woman Denied Morning After Pill by Pharmacist," *Union Leader*, September 27, 2004.

6. Susan Cohen, "A Message to the President: Abortion Can Be Safe, Legal and Still Rare," *Guttmacher Report on Public Policy* 4, no. 1 (February 2001). http://www.guttmacher.org/pubs/tgr/04/1/gr040101.html (accessed November 4, 2004).

7. Alan Guttmacher Institute, "After Three Decades of Legal Abortion, New Research Documents Declines in Rates, Numbers and Access

to Abortion Services," January 15, 2003. http://www.guttmacher.org/media/nr/nr_011003.html (accessed August 19, 2005); Centers for Disease Control and Prevention, "Trends in Pregnancies and Pregnancy Rates by Outcome: Estimates for the United States, 1976–96," *Vital and Health Statistics*, ser. 21, no. 56 (January 2000); Physicians for Reproductive Choice and Health and the Alan Guttmacher Institute, "Abortion in the United States," Power Point presentation. http://www.agi-ny.org/presentations/abort_slides.ppt (accessed September 12, 2005).

8. Alan Guttmacher Institute, "Facts in Brief: Contraceptive Use," 2004. http://www.agi-usa.org/pubs/fb_contr_use.html (accessed February 3, 2005).

9. Ibid.

10. Ibid.

11. American Life League, "Philosophy." http://www.all.org/out/policy2.htm (accessed March 5, 2005); American Life League, "American Life League on the Hidden Abortionists: Searle Pharmaceutical Company to Be Target of Protest," PR Newswire, August 15, 1996.

12. American Life League, "Artificial Contraception: Contrary to God's Plan," chap. 104 of *Pro-Life Activist's Encyclopedia*. http://www.ewtn.com/library/PROLENC/ENCYC104.HTM (accessed December 3, 2004).

13. Naral Pro-Choice America, personal correspondence with author, January 6, 2005.

14. Phil Magers, "Pharmacists Focus of Debate," United Press International, April 5, 2004.

15. Howard Fischer and Stephanie Innes, "Arizona Bill Might Cut Birth Control Access," *Arizona Daily Star*, January 26, 2005. http://www.dailystar.com/dailystar/dailystar/58558.php (accessed March 6, 2005).

16. Americans United for Life, "Health Care Rights of Conscience Legislation." http://www.americansunitedforlife.org/guide/roc/roc_intro.htm (accessed March 6, 2005; emphasis added).

17. David Sackett and others, "Evidence-Based Medicine: What It Is and What It Isn't," *British Medical Journal* 312 (January 13, 1996):

71–72, from Centre for Evidence-Based Medicine. http://www.cebm.net/ebm_is_isnt.asp (accessed March 6, 2005).

18. National Right to Life, "Mission Statement." http://www.nrlc.org/Missionstatement.htm (accessed March 5, 2005).

19. Representative Chris Smith, chair of the Pro-Life Caucus in Congress, claimed on the floor of Congress that various methods of contraception that would be covered by the proposed legislation also cause abortions. Treasury and General Government Appropriations Act, "Correction of *Congressional Record* of July 16, 1998, pages 5719, 5720 and 5721, during Debate on H.R. 4104, Treasury and General Government Appropriations Act, 1999" (House of Representatives, July 20, 1998). http://thomas.loc.gov/cgi-bin/query/F?r105:1:./temp/~r105295jjL:e689: (accessed October 20, 2005).

20. *Congressional Record,* House, H. 10528, "What Is Going on in Congress?" October 11, 1998.

21. John Long, fax to author, March 15, 2005. Hawaii Right to Life testimony by executive director John Long, in opposition to stop HB 1240 HD 1, "Opposition to MB 1240 HD 1 Relating to Emergency Contraception and Abortifacients for Sexual Assault Survivors in Emergency Rooms," February 15, 2005; Rocky Mountain Family Council, Legislative Update, January 28, 2005; Mass Citizens for Life press release, June 29, 2004; EC in the ER legislation opposed by Pro-Life Wisconsin: Hannah Gaedtke, "Legislation Would Require Hospitals to Provide Emergency Contraception," *Badger Herald*, February 20, 2003; EC in the ER legislation opposed by Louisiana Right to Life Federation: Joan Treadway, "Post-rape Birth Control Debated: Religious, Healthcare Concerns Weighed," *Times-Picayune*, March 9, 2003; Florida Right to Life opposed the "Emergency Treatment of Rape Victims" legislation reported on their Web site: "2002 Final Legislative Report." http://www.frtl.org/2002/2002_final_legislative_report.htm (accessed March 6, 2005).

22. John Leland, "Under Abortion Debate Din, an Experience Shared Often but Mentioned Only Quietly," *New York Times*, September 18, 2005.

23. Dr. and Mrs. J. C. Willke, "Health: More Specifically, Mental Health," in *Why Can't We Love Them Both?*" http://www.abortionfacts.

com/online_books/love_them_both/why_cant_we_love_them_both_9_ asp (accessed August 17, 2005).

24. American Psychological Association Online, "American Psychological Association Briefing Paper on the Impact of Abortion on Women." http://www.apa.org/ppo/issues/womenabortfacts.html (accessed January 29, 2005; emphasis added).

25. Ibid.

26. Gallup Organization Poll, Question Profile, "U.S. Catholics," August 5, 1993.

27. William Mosher and others, "Use of Contraception and Use of Family Planning Services in the United States, 1982–2002," *Centers for Disease Control Advance Data from Vital and Health Statistics*, no. 350 (December 10, 2004). http://www.cdc.gov/nchs/data/ad/ad350.pdf (accessed August 11, 2005).

28. Planned Parenthood, "The Equity in Prescription Insurance and Contraceptive Coverage Act." http://www.plannedparenthood.org/pp2/ portal/files/portal/medicalinfo/birthcontrol/fact-prescription-coverage-act.xml (accessed August 11, 2005).

29. Kelley M. Blassingame, "Federal Ruling Reverses Contraceptive Coverage Debate," *Employee Benefit News* 15, no. 10 (August 1, 2001). http://www.benefitnews.com/subscriber/Article.cfm?id=8695 (accessed September 13, 2004).

30. Quote given to reporter: "Bill Would Cover Contraceptives for Ohio Women," June 8, 2004. http://www.channelcincinnati.com/news/ 3396105/detail.html (accessed March 5, 2005).

31. Kim Douglass, "Bill Would Make Insurance Companies Cover the Pill," *Wilmington (DE) News Journal*, May 10, 1999 (emphasis added).

32. Jennifer Coleman, "Measures Require Health Insurers to Cover Birth Control Prescriptions," Associated Press, April 2, 2002.

33. Text of the law "An Act Concerning Insurance Coverage," HB 0211, Illinois 93rd General Assembly.

34. Illinois Right to Life, "2004 Session of the Illinois General Assembly." http://www.ifrl.org/state/index.htm (accessed January 23, 2005).

35. Quote given to reporter: Peter Prengaman, "Birth Control Pills

Won't Be Part of Insurance Coverage," Associated Press State and Local Wire, May 22, 2003.

36. American Life League, "ACOG Is Wrong—Contraception Is Not a 'Medical Necessity,'" PR Newswire, May 11, 1998.

37. Editorial, "Contraceptive Coverage a Must," *Madison (WI) Capital Times,* October 13, 1999.

38. Ray Hartmann, "Misplaced Morality: There's Nothing Holy about the War on Family Planning," *Riverfront Times* (St. Louis, MO), June 6, 2001.

39. Alan Guttmacher Institute, "State Policies in Brief: Insurance Coverage for Contraceptives," 2004.

40. Cindy Schroeder, "Right to Life Adds Pill to List," *Cincinnati Enquirer,* April 26, 2002. http://www.enquirer.com/editions/2002/04/26/loc_right_to_life_adds.html (accessed September 13, 2004).

41. Elizabeth Graham, executive director, Texas Right to Life, e-mail correspondence with author; Texas Right to Life, "State Legislature Questionnaire 2004–2005." http://www.texasrighttolife.com/vote/2004/stateleg0405.htm (accessed January 23, 2005).

42. Couple to Couple League for Natural Family Planning, "Contraception." http://www.ccli.org/contraception/index.shtml (accessed March 5, 2005).

43. Illinois Federation for Right to Life, "Chemical Abortion." http://www.ifrl.org/topic/chemical/ (accessed November 12, 2004).

44. Iowa Right to Life Committee, "Glossary of Abortifacients." http://www.irlc.org/medical/m_abortifacients.htm (accessed November 12, 2004).

45. Wisconsin Right to Life, http://www.wrtl.org/women_birthcontrol.htm (accessed December 2, 2004). Web site now altered from original claim. Mike Froncek, communications coordinator, Wisconsin Right to Life, personal e-mail correspondence with author, December 29, 2004.

46. Missionairies to the Preborn, "Everything You Never Wanted to Know about Birth Control: A Guide for Engaged and Newlywed Couples." http://www.missionariestopreborn.com/default.asp?fuseaction=bc_newlyweds (accessed March 5, 2005).

47. Army of God, "Anti-Abortion Heroes of Faith." http://www.army ofgod.com/heroes.html (accessed October 20, 2005).

48. Army of God, "Is Birth Control the Same as Aborting Babies?" http://armyofgod.com/birthcontrol.html (accessed October 20, 2005).

49. Army of God. http://www.armyofgod.com (accessed December 19, 2004).

50. American College of Obstetricians and Gynecologists, "Statement on Contraceptive Methods," July 1998. "Essential steps necessary for pregnancy include . . . implantation of the blastocyst into the lining of the uterus at the conclusion of which pregnancy is established."

51. Department of Health and Human Services, Code of Federal Regulations, Title 45, 46.203(f), p. 116.

52. Roberto Rivera, MD, Irene Yacobson, MD, and David Grimes, "The Mechanism of Action of Hormonal Contraceptives and Intrauterine Contraceptive Devices," *American Journal of Obstetrics and Gynecology* 181 (1999): 1263–1269.

53. Statement by twenty-two pro-life physicians. Watson Bowes and others, "Prolife Ob/Gyn's January 1998 Statement: Birth Control Pills: Contraceptive or Abortifacient," from Eternal Perspective Ministries. http://www.epm.org/articles/doctors.html (accessed March 11, 2005).

54. David Grimes, personal e-mail correspondence with author, March 11, 2005.

55. Physicians for Life, "Condoms & STDs." http://www.physicians forlife.org/content/category/11/135/36/ (accessed March 5, 2005).

56. Pamphlet produced by the American Life League, *Answers to Your Questions about Condoms and Spermicides* (2004).

57. Alan Guttmacher Institute, "Facts in Brief: Contraceptive Use," 2005.

58. Angela R. Baerwald, B. Sc. Hon., Gregg P. Adams, DVM, MS, PhD, and Roger A. Pierson, MS, PhD, "A New Model for Ovarian Follicular Development during the Human Menstrual Cycle," *Fertility and Sterility* 80, no. 1 (July 2003): 116–122.

59. Sharon Kirkey, "'Flabbergasted' Scientists Find They've Been Wrong on Ovulation," *CanWest News Service*, July 8, 2003.

60. American Life League, "American Life League on the Hidden Abortionists."

61. Marie Costa, *Contemporary World Issues: Abortion* (Santa Barbara, CA: ABC-CLIO, 1991), 53.

62. Guidestar, the national database of nonprofit organizations. http://www.guidestar.org/controller/searchResults.gs?action_gsReport=1&npoId=195503 (accessed March 5, 2005).

63. *The Pro-Life Activist's Encyclopedia*, published by the American Life League, is available on the Eternal World Television Network Web site at http://www.ewtn.com (accessed August 17, 2005).

64. American Life League, "Artificial Contraception: Contrary to God's Plan," chap. 104 of *Pro-Life Activist's Encyclopedia*. http://www.ewtn.com/library/PROLENC/ENCYC104.HTM (accessed December 3, 2004).

65. American Life League, "Philosophy." http://www.all.org/about/policy2.htm (accessed August 17, 2005).

66. Mary Leonard, "Fight Goes on for U.S. Worker's Coverage: Supporters Push Effort for Contraceptive Refunds," *Boston Globe*, October 9, 1998.

67. American Life League, "House Birth Control Vote a Major Victory for Life," PR Newswire, October 8, 1998.

68. American Life League, "American Life League on the Hidden Abortionists."

69. American Life League, "A.L.L.—Introduction: The Abortion-Contraception Connection," chap. 97 of *Pro-Life Activist's Encyclopedia;* "Chapter 90," *Pro-Life Activist's Encyclopedia*. http://www.ewtn.com/library/PROLENC/ENCYC097.HTM (accessed August 17, 2005).

70. American Life League, "American Life League on the Hidden Abortionists."

Chapter Two

1. ABC News, "The American Sex Survey: A Peek beneath the Sheets," ABC News/*PrimeTime Live* poll, October 21, 2004.

2. Randall Terry, "Why Do Christians Use Birth Control?" *Life Advocate Magazine*, 1997. http://www.lifeadvocate.org/arc/terry.htm (accessed September 17, 2005).

3. Linda Witt, "Man with a Mission: Joe Scheidler Pulls No Punches in Crusade against Abortion," *Chicago Tribune*, August 11, 1985.

4. Jennifer Warner, "What Makes Women Happy? Sex Tops List: New Tool Measuring Happiness Shows Women Enjoy Sex Most, Commuting Least," *WebMD Medical News*, December 9, 2004.

5. Elizabeth Querna, "Special Report: Cover Package—50 Ways to Fix Your Life," *U.S. News and World Report* 137, no. 23 (December 27, 2004): 60.

6. Alice Park, "Sexual Healing: What Feels Good Is Good for You Too; Making Love Can Boost the Heart, Relieve Pain, and Help Keep You Healthy," *Time*, January 19, 2004.

7. Jared Diamond, *Why Is Sex Fun? The Evolution of Human Sexuality* (New York: Basic Books, 1997), 68.

8. *Self*, April 2005.

9. *Men's Health*, April 2005.

10. "Happily Unmarried: How-to from a Guidebook for Couples Living Together without Saying 'I Do,'" *Time*, March 3, 2003.

11. Theodore Caplow, Louis Hicks, and Ben J. Wattenberg, *The First Measured Century: An Illustrated Guide to Trends in America, 1900–2000* (Washington, DC: American Enterprise Institute, 2001), 74.

12. Alfred Lubrano, "Greeting Cards for Cheaters: Adultery, Always Hot, Is Now Pop-Cult Caliente; This Line of Love Missives Is for Sealing with Illicit Kisses," *Philadelphia Inquirer*, August 25, 2005.

13. Margaret Sanger authored *Happiness in Marriage* in 1926. Marie Stopes wrote *Married Love* in 1918.

14. Ellen Chesler, *Woman of Valor: Margaret Sanger and the Birth Control Movement in America* (New York: Simon and Schuster, 1992), 14.

15. "Birth Control," *Time*, December 17, 1923.

16. Katherine Bement Davis, *Factors in the Sex Life of Twenty-two Hundred Women* (New York: Harper and Brothers, 1929), 357, 376, 377.

17. Stephanie Coontz, *The Way We Never Were: American Families and the Nostalgia Trap* (New York: Basic Books, 1992), 39.

18. Ibid., 25–26.

19. Ibid., 29.

20. Ibid., 30.

21. Ibid., 32.

22. Ibid.

23. Ibid.

24. Ibid., 36.

25. Ibid.

26. Gallup Poll News Service, "The Most Important Events of the Century from the Viewpoint of the People," December 6, 1999. http://www.gallup.com/poll/content/print.aspx?ci=3427 (accessed February 27, 2005).

27. National Center for Health Statistics, "American Women Are Waiting to Begin Families," December 11, 2002. http://www.cdc.gov/nchs/pressroom/02news/ameriwomen.htm (accessed December 27, 2005).

28. National Center for Education Statistics, "Fast Facts: Title IX." http://nces.ed.gov/fastfacts/display.asp?id=93 (accessed April 7, 2005).

29. Alison Szot, "Women Even the Odds: Healthcare Isn't an 'Old Boys' Network Anymore, as Women Catch up to Men in Leadership Positions," *Modern Healthcare*, April 18, 2005; "Education Degrees and Tenure Awarded to Women," Women's Health USA 2005, Health Resources and Services Administration; "A Current Glance of Women and the Law," American Bar Association, Commission on Women in the Profession.

30. Claudia Goldin and Lawrence F. Katz, "The Power of the Pill: Oral Contraceptives and Women's Career and Marriage Decisions," *Journal of Political Economy* 110, no. 4 (2002): 730–770.

31. Anna Fels, *Necessary Dreams: Ambition in Women's Changing Lives* (New York: Anchor Books, 2004), 205.

32. U.S. Department of Labor, Bureau of Labor Statistics. http://www.bls.gov.

33. James T. Bond and others, "Highlights of the National Study of the Changing Workforce: Women in the Workforce," *Families and Work Institute*, no. 3 (2002): 1.

34. U.S. Census Bureau, "Poverty: Historical Poverty Tables." http://www.census.gov/hhes/www/poverty/histpov/hstpov2.html (accessed September 28, 2005).

35. Kristin Anderson Moore, PhD, and Zakia Redd, MPP, "Children in Poverty: Trends, Consequences, and Policy Options," *Child Trends Research Brief* (November 2002).

36. National Opinion Research Center, University of Chicago, "General Social Survey 2002," February 2002, I-Poll databank. http://roper/center.uconn.edu.

37. Centers for Disease Control, "Births: Final Data for 2002," *National Vital Statistics Reports* 52, no. 10 (December 17, 2003); Coontz, *Way We Never Were*, 39.

38. Bond and others, "Highlights of the National Study," 4.

39. Lydia Sand, "Women See Room for Improvement in Job Equity but Are Generally Satisfied with Their Lives," *Gallup News Service*, June 29, 2001. http://www.gallup.com/poll/content/print/aspx?ci=4561 (accessed February 27, 2005).

40. Fels, *Necessary Dreams*, 206.

41. "Mothers at Work: For Many Women, a Commitment to Family Values Means Working Outside the Home," *Bismarck (ND) Tribune*, August 18, 1996.

42. Ed Hayward and Tom Mashberg, "Upheaval in '80s Put the Spotlight on Child Abuse," *Boston Herald*, December 3, 1995.

43. Ibid.

44. Ibid.

45. Ibid.

46. "Mothers at Work."

47. Janice Shaw Crouse, "The Cost of 'Having It All,'" April 28, 2005. http://www.townhall.com/columnists/GuestColumns/Crouse20050428.shtml (accessed August 18, 2005).

48. U.S. Senate roll-call votes, 103rd Cong., 1st sess., for each senator's voting record and position on choice. http://www.issues2000.org and Naral Pro-Choice America.

49. Ibid. Based on the voting records of the twenty-seven senators who voted against the Family Medical Leave Act, twenty-four are "pro-life." They are Bennett, Brown, Cochran, Coverdell, Craig, Dole, Domenici, Faircloth, Gorton, Gramm, Grasley, Gregg, Hatch, Heflin, Helms, Kempthorne, Lott, Lugar, Mack, McConnell, Mickles, Pressler, Smith, and Warner; the others are Hollings, Kassebaum, and Simpson.

50. Children's Defense Fund, "How Well Do Your Members of Congress Protect Children? The 2004 Children's Defense Fund Action Council Nonpartisan Congressional Scorecard." http://www.cdfaction council.org/scorecard/2004.pdf (accessed August 22, 2005). The Children's Defense Fund's "best" and "worst" legislators' positions on abortion comes from http://issues2000.org and Naral Pro-Choice America.

51. Ibid.

52. Jean Reith Schroedel, *Is the Fetus a Person? A Comparison of Policies across the Fifty States* (Ithaca, NY: Cornell University Press, 2000), 148.

53. Ibid., 157.

54. Ibid., 156.

55. Rob Boston, "If Best-Selling End-Times Author Tim LaHaye Has His Way, Church-State Separation Will Be . . . Left Behind," Americans United for Separation of Church and State Web site, February 2002. http://www.au.org/site/News2?page=NewsArticle&id=5601&abbr=cs_ (accessed September 19, 2005).

56. Laurie Goodstein, "At Work, Pro-Family Groups Vary Balance of Home, Job," *Washington Post*, July 28, 1997.

57. Illinois Right to Life Committee, news briefs from third quarter 2003. http://www.illinoisrighttolife.org/RecentNews03third.htm (accessed April 23, 2005).

58. Brian Robertson, "Day Care Deception: The Family under Siege—

August 19, 2003," Family Policy Lecture, Family Research Council. http://www.frc.org/get.cfm?i=PL04C03 (accessed September 18, 2005).

59. Sheryl Gay Stolberg, "Public Lives: Another Academic Salvo in the Nation's 'Mommy Wars,'" *New York Times*, April 21, 2001.

60. "Balancing Family, Work Day-Care Study Raises Questions, and Anxious Moms Need Answers," *USA Today*, May 3, 2001.

61. Jennifer Foote Sweeney, "Jay Belsky Doesn't Play Well with Others," Salon.com, members-only archive, April 26, 2001.

62. Jay Belsky, interview by author, May 10, 2005.

63. Kate Lorenz, "Equal Pay for Women? Not till 2050." http://www.cnn.com/2004/us/careers/10/22/equal.pay/index.html (accessed November 11, 2004).

64. Peter Cattan, "The Effect of Working Wives on the Incidence of Poverty," *Monthly Labor Review* (March 1998): 22–29.

65. U.S. Census Bureau, 1998; Planned Parenthood Federation of America, "*Griswold v. Connecticut:* The Impact of Legal Birth Control and the Challenges That Remain." http://www.plannedparenthood.org/pp2/portal/file/portal/medicalinfo/birthcontrol/fact–0005101-griswold-done.xml (accessed August 19, 2005).

66. Darren K. Carlson, "Just about Half of Adult Americans Are Currently Married but Only about One-Fifth Have Never Been Married," *Gallup Poll News Service*, February 1, 2001. http://www.gallup.com/poll/content/print.aspx?ci=2053 (accessed February 27, 2005).

67. Federal Interagency Forum on Child and Family Statistics, "America's Children: Key National Indicators of Well-Being, 2002," 18. http://www.childstats.gov/americaschildren/pdf/ac2002/econ.pdf (accessed August 22, 2005).

68. New York University, "Study Offers First Glimpse of How Income Affects Pre-Schoolers' Cognitive Abilities and Behavior: NYU Sociologist and Columbia Colleagues Identify Distinct Mechanisms for Income's Effect on Achievement and Behavior," press release, November 12, 2002. http://www.nyu.edu/publicaffairs/newsreleases/b_STUDY.shtml (accessed June 15, 2005).

69. Childtrends Databank, "Reading to Young Children." http://www. childtrendsdatabank.org/indicators/5ReadingtoYoungChildren.cfm (accessed August 25, 2005).

70. John F. Sandberg and Sandra L. Hofferth, *Changes in Children's Time with Parents, U.S. 1981–1997*, report no. 01–475 (Ann Arbor: Population Studies Center, the Institute for Social Research, University of Michigan, May 2001).

71. Bond and others, "Highlights of the National Study," 4.

72. Sandberg and Hofferth, *Changes in Children's Time.*

73. Tasneem A. Grace, "Father Time No Longer Stuck in Tradition: Dads Enjoy Their Kids More than Ever," *Syracuse Post-Standard,* June 21, 1998.

74. U.S. Census Bureau, 1998; Planned Parenthood Federation of America, "*Griswold v. Connecticut:* The Impact."

75. Roger Bull, "Generation Dad: Fathers, Kids Both Benefit from Interaction," *Jacksonville Florida Times-Union,* June 20, 1999.

76. Spike TV, "Men's State of the Union Overview," March 14–21, 2004.

77. Philip Elmer-Dewitt, "The Great Experiment: Today's Parents Are Raising Their Children in Ways That Little Resemble Their Own Youth; The Question That Haunts Them: Will the Kids Be All Right?" *Time,* November 8, 1990.

78. Liz Stevens, "Think Guys Are Tough? They're Competitive? They Don't Eat Quiche, and They Don't Cry? Think Again, Say Experts. A New Man Is on the Horizon. He's Sensitive. He's . . . Man. Kinder," *Fort Worth (TX) Star-Telegram,* December 5, 1999.

79. Justin Davidson, "The Changing Man: A Picture of Fatherhood Evolving," *New York Newsday,* June 13, 2002.

80. "National Survey Shows Fathers Are Hugging Children More: UC Riverside Sociologists Say Involved Fathers Set a Good Example," AScribe Newswire, June 13, 2002.

81. Grace, "Father Time."

82. Ibid.

83. Sand, "Women See Room for Improvement."

84. "National Men's Study Conducted by Spike TV Reveals Conflict in Male Self Identity Featured Exclusively in TIME Magazine," PR Newswire, August 15, 2004.

85. Ibid.

86. Gallup Poll News Service, "1997 Global Study of Family Values," November 7, 1997. http://www.gallup.com/poll/content/print.aspx?ci=9871 (accessed September 1, 2005).

Chapter Three

1. Alan Guttmacher Institute, "Abortion in Context: United States and Worldwide," *Issues in Brief.* http://www.guttmacher.org/pubs/ib_0599.html (accessed July 6, 2005).

2. Leslie Reagan, *When Abortion Was a Crime* (Berkeley and Los Angeles: University of California Press, 1997), 7.

3. Ibid., 23.

4. Department of the Interior, *Report on Population of the United States at the Eleventh Census, 1890* (Washington, DC: Government Printing Office, 1895). http://www.census.gov/prod/www/abs/decennial/1890.htm (accessed August 24, 2005); U.S. Bureau of the Census, "U.S. and World Population Clocks-POPClocks." http://www.census.gov/main/www/popclock.html (accessed August 24, 2005).

5. Reagan, *When Abortion Was a Crime,* 23.

6. Rachel K. Jones, Jacqueline E. Darroch, and Stanley K. Henshaw, "Patterns in the Socioeconomic Characteristics of Women Obtaining Abortions in 2000–2001," *Perspectives on Sexual and Reproductive Health* 34, no. 5 (September–October 2002): 226–235.

7. Ibid.

8. Alan Guttmacher Institute, "Mandatory Counseling and Waiting Period for Abortion," *State Policies in Brief* (June 1, 2005).

9. Physicians for Reproductive Choice and Health and the Alan

Guttmacher Institute, "An Overview of Abortion in the United States," June 2005. http://www.guttmacher.org/presentations/abort_slides.pdf (accessed September 25, 2005).

10. Ted Joyce and Robert Kaestner, "The Impact of Mississippi's Mandatory Delay Law on the Timing of Abortion," *Family Planning Perspectives* 32, no. 1 (January–February 2000): 4–13.

11. Stanley Henshaw, "The Impact of Requirements for Parental Consent on Minors' Abortions in Mississippi," *Family Planning Perspectives* 27, no. 3 (May–June 1995): 120–122.

12. Ted Joyce and Robert Kaestner, "Changes in Abortion and Births Following Texas's Parental Notification Statute: A Regression Discontinuity Approach" (forthcoming).

13. Naral Pro-Choice Texas, "Political Updates: 79th Legislative Session." http://www.prochoicetexas.org/s04politicalupdates/ (accessed July 6, 2005).

14. Patricia Donovan, *Our Daughters' Decisions: The Conflict in State Law on Abortion and Other Issues* (New York: Alan Guttmacher Institute, 1992), 21.

15. Physicians for Reproductive Choice and Health and the Alan Guttmacher Institute, "Overview of Abortion."

16. Willard Cates Jr., David A. Grimes, and Kenneth F. Schultz, "The Public Health Impact of Legal Abortion: 30 Years Later," *Perspectives on Sexual and Reproductive Health* 35, no. 1 (January–February 2003): 25–28.

17. Alan Guttmacher Institute, "Induced Abortion in the United States," *Facts in Brief* (2005).

18. Ibid.

19. National Abortion Federation, "Facts about Mifepristone (RU-486)." http://www.prochoice.org/pubs_research/publications/downloads/about_abortion/facts_about_mifepristone.html (accessed August 19, 2005).

20. Norma Peterson, "RU-486 and Breast Cancer," *Breast Cancer Action*, newsletter 10 (February 1992). http://www.bcaction.org/Pages/

SearchablePages/1992Newsletter/Newsletter010A.html (accessed June 18, 2005).

21. The National Academies, "Potential Benefits of RU–486, Other Antiprogestins Are Extensive," press release, September 9, 1993. http://www4.nationalacademies.org/news.nsf/isbn/0309049490?Open Document (accessed June 19, 2005).

22. "First Trial Open to Examines Mifepristone in Treatment of Endometrial Cancer," *CancerWise* (February 2002). http://www.cancer wise.org/february_2002/ (accessed June 18, 2005), which also discusses potential in treating ovarian and prostate cancers; National Institute of Mental Health, "Clinical Trial of Mifepristone for Bipolar Depression." http://www.clinicaltrials.gov/show/NCT00043654 (accessed June 18, 2005); Johns Hopkins Medical School, "Hopkins Researchers Use RU–486 to Treat Brain Tumors," press release, September 21, 1994. http://www.hopkinsmedicine.org/press/1994/SEPT/19949.HTM (accessed June 18, 2005); Contraception Report, "Mifepristone: Emergency Contraception and Other Uses," vol. 11, December 2000. http://www. contraceptiononline.org/contrareport/article01.cfm?art=109 (accessed June 19, 2005); Feminist Majority Foundation, "Feminist Majority Foundation Reports on Mifepristone: A Chronology in Brief." http://www. feminist.org/welcome/ru486one.html (accessed June 18, 2005).

23. Feminist Majority Foundation, "Feminist Majority Foundation Reports on Mifepristone."

24. "CWA Joins Press Conference to Herald Legislation to Suspend FDA's Approval of RU-486," U.S. Newswire, November 5, 2003.

25. National Abortion Federation, "Medical Abortion Safety Information," December 8, 2004.

26. Ibid.

27. Save the Children, "Children Having Children: State of the World's Mothers, 2004," May 2004, 31.

28. National Abortion Federation, "Medical Abortion Safety Information."

29. Alan Guttmacher Institute, "Induced Abortion in the United States."

30. Ibid.

31. Alan Guttmacher Institute, "Sex Education: Needs, Programs and Policies," July 2005. http://www.guttmacher.org/presentations/sex_ed.pdf (accessed August 27, 2005).

32. Hannah Bruckner and Peter Bearman, "After the Promise: The STD Consequences of Adolescent Virginity Pledges," *Journal of Adolescent Health* 36, no. 4 (April 2005): 271–278.

33. Ibid.

34. Ibid.

35. Debra Hauser, MPH, "Five Years of Abstinence-Only-Until-Marriage Education: Assessing the Impact," *Title V State Evaluations*, Advocates for Youth, 2004. http://www.advocatesforyouth.org/publications/stateevaluations/.

36. SIECUS Public Policy Office, "What the Research Says . . . ," SIECUS Public Policy Office Fact Sheet. http://www.siecus.org/policy/research_says.pdf.

37. Ibid.

38. The National Campaign to Prevent Teen Pregnancy, "Teen Sexual Activity in the United States, 2003."

39. Hauser, "Five Years."

40. Ibid.

41. Advocates for Youth, "Science or Politics? George W. Bush and the Future of Sexuality Education in the United States." http://www.advocatesforyouth.org/publications/factsheet/fsbush.htm (accessed July 6, 2005).

42. Human Rights Watch, "Ignorance Only: HIV/AIDS, Human Rights and Federally Funded Abstinence-Only Programs in the United States, Texas: A Case Study," *Human Rights Watch* 14, no. 5 (G) (September 2002): 8.

43. Ibid., 21.

44. Ibid., 24.

45. Advocates for Youth, "Science or Politics?"

46. Government Reform Minority Office, "The Effectiveness of Abstinence-Only Education," in *Politics and Science: Investigating the State of*

Science under the Bush Administration. http://democrats.reform.house.
gov/features/politics_and_science/example_abstinence.htm (accessed
June 9, 2005).

47. Douglas Kirby, *Emerging Answers: Research Findings on Programs
to Reduce Teen Pregnancy* (Washington, DC: National Campaign to Prevent Teen Pregnancy, 2001), 78.

48. Susan Philliber, "Building Evaluation into Your Work," in *Get Organized: A Guide to Preventing Teen Pregnancy* (Washington, DC: National Campaign to Prevent Teen Pregnancy, 2001). http://aspe.hhs.
gov/hsp/get-organized99/ch16/pdf (accessed August 23, 2005), 136.

49. Union of Concerned Scientists, "Scientific Knowledge on Abstinence-Only Education Distorted," from *Scientific Integrity in Policymaking*, 2004, and CDC, Programs That Work (archived version available
online at http://web.archive.org/web/20010606142729/www.cdc.gov/
nccdphp/dash/rtc/index.htm).

50. Ibid., http://www.ucsusa.org/global_environment/rsi/page.cfm?
pageIID=1355 (accessed December 29, 2004).

51. Ceci Connolly, "Administration Promoting Abstinence; Family
Planning Efforts Are Being Scaled Back," *Washington Post,* July 30,
2001.

52. Robert O. Bothwell and Kay Guinane, "Continuing Attacks on
Nonprofit Speech: Death by a Thousand Cuts II," *OMB Watch* (October
2004): 10.

53. Ibid.

54. Christopher Healy, "No Sex, Please—or We'll Audit You,"
Salon.com, October 28, 2003.

55. E-mail correspondence with Adrienne Verilli, director of communications for SIECUS, August 23, 2005.

56. Sexuality Information and Education Council of the United States,
"State Funding by Number of and Amount Given to Crisis Pregnancy
Centers/Anti-Choice Organizations." Provided to the author by the orga-
nization.

57. SIECUS, "Federal Spending for Abstinence-Only-Until-Marriage

Programs (1982–2006)." http://www.siecus.org/policy/states/2004/federalGraph.html (accessed August 27, 2005).

58. People for the American Way, "Teaching Fear: The Religious Right's Campaign against Sexuality Education." http://www.pfaw.org/pfaw/general/default.aspx?oid=2024&print=yes&units=all (accessed August 19, 2005).

59. Warren King, "Anti-condom Ad Distorted, Health Officials Complain," *Seattle Times*, May 26, 1993.

60. "Condom-Pushers Say Having More Money than Abstinence Programs Isn't Enough—They Want It All," Abstinence Clearinghouse press release, U.S. Newswire, March 8, 2005.

61. Abstinence Clearinghouse, "About Us." http://abstinence.net/about/history.php (accessed August 19, 2005).

62. Ibid.

63. Cynthia Gorney, "Abortion in the Heartland: For Women in South Dakota, There's Only One Doctor to Call," *Washington Post*, October 2, 1990.

64. David Kranz, "Leslee Unruh Has Been a Guest on *Oprah*, Invited to the White House and Urged to Run for Office: The Founder of the Alpha Center Has Become a National . . . ," *Argus Leader* (Sioux Falls, SD), July 20, 2003.

65. *Sex Education in America* (Washington, DC: National Public Radio, Henry J. Kaiser Family Foundation, and Kennedy School of Government, 2004), 7.

66. "The Content of Federally Funded Abstinence-Only Education Programs," prepared for Representative Henry Waxman, United States House of Representatives Committee on Government Reform—Minority Staff, Special Investigations Division, December 2004, i.

67. Ibid.

68. Ibid., 14.

69. Ibid., 21.

70. Ibid., i.

71. Ibid.

72. Ibid., ii.

73. Ibid., 8.

74. Ibid., ii.

75. Ibid.

76. United States District Court for the Eastern District of Louisiana, *American Civil Liberties Union of Louisiana v. Governor M. J. Foster and Dan Richey*, Memorandum of Law in Support of Motion for Preliminary Injunction, 4. http://www.aclu.org/Files/OpenFile.cfm?id=13579.

77. Ibid., 12.

78. Ibid.

79. ACLU, "ACLU Asks Court to Hold Louisiana's Abstinence-Only Program in Contempt, Citing Numerous Violations of 2002 Order," press release, January 20, 2005. http://www.aclu.org/Reproductive Rights/ReproductiveRights.cfm?ID=17343&c=30 (accessed May 18, 2005).

80. United States District Court for the District of Massachusetts, *American Civil Liberties Union of Massachusetts v. Leavitt*. http://www. aclu.org/Files/getFile.cfm?id=18241.

81. Ibid.

82. Ibid.

83. BBC, *American Virgins*, transcript, 10.31.15–10.31.33, January 25, 2004. http://news.bbc.co.uk/1/shared/spl/hi/programmes/correspondent/transcripts/american_virgins_250104.txt (accessed June 8, 2005).

84. Ibid., 10.31.51–10.31.57.

85. United States District Court for the District of Massachusetts, *American Civil Liberties Union of Massachusetts v. Leavitt*.

86. American Civil Liberties Union, "ACLU Applauds Federal Government's Decision to Suspend Funding of Religion by Nationwide Abstinence-Only-Until-Marriage Program," August 22, 2005. http://www. aclu.org/ReproductiveRights/ReproductiveRights.cfm?ID=18941&c= 30 (accessed September 30, 2005).

87. David J. Landry, Lisa Kaeser, and Cory L. Richards, "Abstinence

Promotion and the Provision of Information about Contraception in Public School District Sexuality Education Policies," *Family Planning Perspectives* 31, no. 6 (1999): 280–286.

88. The National Campaign to Prevent Teen Pregnancy, "Teen Pregnancy and Birth Rates in the United States," February 2004. http://www.teenpregnancy.org/resources/data/pdf/STBYST905.pdf.

89. Southern State AIDS/STD Directors Work Group, "Southern States Manifesto HIV/SIDS & STDs in the South: A Call to Action," March 2, 2003. http://www.hivdent.org/manifesto.pdf (accessed August 23, 2005), 9.

90. Ibid.

91. Ibid., 6.

92. UNICEF, "A League Table of Teenage Births in Rich Nations," *Innoocenti Report Card,* no. 3 (July 2001): 4–5. http://www.unicef-icdc.org/publications/pdf/repcard3e.pdf (accessed August 23, 2005).

93. Ibid., 6.

94. Alan Guttmacher Institute, "Into a New World: Young Women's Sexual and Reproductive Lives," 2005. http://www.guttmacher.org/pubs/new_world_engl.html (accessed August 28, 2005).

95. UNICEF, "League Table," 20–21.

96. Ibid., 21.

97. Ibid.

98. Ibid.

99. Ibid.

100. Ibid.

101. Ibid., 11.

102. "Administration Promoting Abstinence," *Washington Post,* July 30, 2001.

103. Alan Guttmacher Institute, "Title X: Three Decades of Accomplishment," *Issues in Brief* (2001).

104. W. Mosher and others, "Use of Contraception and Use of Family Planning Services in the U.S., 1982–2002," December 10, 2004. http://www.cdc.gov/nchs/data/ad/ad350.pdf.

105. CATCHUM Project, "Problem Base Learning Task Force-Individual Members: Alma L. Golden M.D., FAAP, MPH." http://www.catchum.utmb.edu/taskforce/fac-dev/fac-dev-member-golden.htm (accessed August 24, 2005).

106. National Family Planning and Reproductive Health Association, "Title X (Ten) National Family Planning Program: Critical Women's Health Program Struggles to Meet Increasing Demand," May 2005.

107. "Title X (Ten), the National Family Planning Program: Provides Essential HIV/AIDS Screening and Prevention Services." http://www.nfprha.org/uploads/TitleXandHIVFactSheet.doc (accessed August 28, 2005).

108. Mark Sherman, "Abstinence Programs Present False, Misleading Information, Lawmaker Says," Associated Press, December 2, 2004.

109. Diana Jean Schemo, "Virginity Pledges by Teenagers Can Be Highly Effective, Federal Study Finds," *New York Times*, January 4, 2001.

Chapter Four

1. Centers for Disease Control and Prevention, "Background on the Weller Study," press release, January 1, 1997. http://aidsinfo.nih.gov/aprs/aprs_press.asp?an=A00351 (accessed June 15, 2001).

2. Dr. Susan Weller, e-mail correspondence to author, June 8, 2005.

3. CDC, "Background on the Weller Study."

4. CDC Divisions of HIV/AIDS Prevention, "Fact Sheet for Public Health Personnel: Male Latex Condoms and Sexually Transmitted Diseases." http://www.cdc.gov/hiv/pubs/facts/condoms.htm (accessed August 23, 2005).

5. National Institute of Allergy and Infectious Diseases, "Workshop Summary: Scientific Evidence on Condom Effectiveness for Sexually Transmitted Disease Prevention: June 12–13, 2000," July 20, 2001, 14, 27. http://www.niaid.nih.gov/dmid/stds/condomreport.pdf.

6. SIECUS, "The Truth about Condoms." http://www.siecus.org/pubs/fact/fact0011.html (accessed August 23, 2005).

7. "The Content of Federally Funded Abstinence-Only Education Programs," prepared for Representative Henry Waxman, United States House of Representatives Committee of Government Reform—Minority Staff, Special Investigations Division, December 2004.

8. Pro-Life America, "Condom Warnings: Beware!" http://www. prolife.com/CONDOMS.html (accessed August 20, 2005).

9. United for Life, "Could Condoms Leak HIV?" http://www.united forlife.com/condomhiv2.html (accessed August 20, 2005).

10. Heritage House: "Condoms: Do They Really Work?" http://www. abortionfacts.com/literature/literature_9331cd.asp (accessed August 20, 2005).

11. Brian Clowes, PhD, "How the Condom Fails at Preventing Transmission of the HIV Virus," Human Life International. http://www.hli. org/bbc_condom-effectiveness.html (accessed June 24, 2005).

12. Physicians for Life, "Physicians Series Brochure: Safe Sex." http://www.physiciansforlife.org/content/view/344/27 (accessed August 20, 2005).

13. National Association of Catholic Families, "Condoms—a Step in the Wrong Direction." http://www.catholic-family.org/documents/ Clovis04.htm (accessed August 20, 2005).

14. Concerned Women for America, "Medical Diagnosis: Condoms Are Full of Holes." http://www.cultureandfamily.org/articledisplay.asp? id=139&department=CFI&categoryid=cfreport (accessed August 20, 2005).

15. American Life League, "The Flawed Condom: Spotting the Big Holes in Condom Propaganda, All the facts You Need to Make an Open-and-Shut Case against the Pro-condom Crowd," 2002.

16. Abstinence Africa, "Welcome to abstinenceAFRICA.org!" http:// www.abstinenceafrica.com/ (accessed August 22, 2005).

17. CIA Worldfact Book (http://www.cia.gov/cia/publications/ factbook/index.html) on HIV/AIDs rates in the countries in which Abstinence Clearinghouse claims to have "affiliates" (as appeared on their Web site, http://www.abstinenceafrica.com/, as of July 20, 2005): Botswana, Cameroon, Egypt, Eritrea, Ethiopia, Ghana, Ivory Coast, Kenya,

Lesotho, Liberia, Libya, Malawi, Nigeria, Rwanda, Sierra Leone, South Africa, Sudan, Swaziland, Tanzania, Uganda, West Africa, Zambia, and Zimbabwe.

18. Alfonso Cardinal Lopez Trujillo, "Family Values versus Safe Sex," *Faith Magazine* (May–June 2005). http://www.faith.org/uk/Publications/ OldMags/mayjun05/faMaJu05.htm (accessed August 20, 2005).

19. BBC News, "Condoms: The Science," June 27, 2004. http://news. bbc.co.uk/1/hi/programmes/panorama/3845011/stm (accessed October 15, 2004).

20. United for Life, "Could Condoms Leak HIV?" http://www.united forlife.com/condomhiv2.html (accessed August 20, 2005).

21. Pro-Life America, "Condom Warnings: Beware!"

22. Physicians for Life, "Safe Sex." http://www.physiciansforlife.org/ content/view/267/58/ (accessed September 26, 2005).

23. American Life League, "Flawed Condom."

24. 100% Pro-Life PAC, "Tom Coburn, MD." http://www.prolifepac. com/html/cancoburn.htm (accessed May 30, 2005).

25. Ron Jenkins, "Coburn Different Kind of Political Cat," Associated Press, July 12, 2004.

26. Ilka Couto and Cynthia Dailard, "Wanted: A Balanced Policy and Program Response to HPV and Cervical Cancer," *Guttmacher Report on Public Policy* 2, no. 6 (December 1999).

27. Ibid.

28. Ibid.

29. Ibid.

30. American Social Health Association, "Information to Live By: Human Papillomavirus (HPV)." http://www.ashastd.org/stdfaqs/hpv.html (accessed June 25, 2005).

31. National Institute of Allergy and Infectious Diseases, "Workshop Summary," ii.

32. Ibid., 26.

33. Susan Okie, "Experts Fear Condom Report's Effects; Panel's Criticism May Deter Some Prophylactic Use, Officials Say," *Washington Post*, July 21, 2001.

34. "CDC: Physicians, Politicians Seek Chief's Resignation," *American Health Line*, July 25, 2001.

35. James Kirley, "Weldon: Condom Effectiveness Being Overplayed; A Report Recently Issued by the U.S. Department of Health and Human Services Found That Existing Epidemiology Literature Was Inadequate to Determine Condom Effectiveness in All but Two Instances," *Press Journal* (August 6, 2001).

36. Kate Leishman, "Controversy and Need for Study on Condoms," United Press International, July 27, 2001.

37. "CDC: Physicians, Politicians Seek Resignation."

38. Ibid.

39. Martha Irvine, "Fretting over the Fine Print: Rending Changes in Condom Labeling Spark Debate," Associated Press Worldstream, April 1, 2004.

40. Laura Meckler, "CDC Fact Sheet Not Promoting Condom Use Any More," Associated Press, December 18, 2002.

41. Lara Jakes Jordan, "Bush Administration Weighs Condom Warning," Associated Press, March 11, 2004.

42. "CDC: Koplan to Resign as Director Next Month," *American Health Line*, February 22, 2002.

43. "Politics and Science: Investigating the State of Science under the Bush Administration," Government Reform Minority Office. http://democrats.reform.house.gov/features/politics_and_science/example_condoms.htm (accessed September 26, 2005).

44. Michelle Goldberg, "Bush's Sex Fantasy," Salon.com, February 24, 2004.

45. Ibid.

46. Ibid.

47. Stephen Foley, "The Challenge: To End Cervical Cancer; The Prize: A Pounds 40BN Drugs Market," *Independent*, December 15, 2004.

48. "Cervical Cancer: HPV Vaccine Shown to 'Substantially' Reduce Cervical Cancer," *Cancer Vaccine Week*, November 29, 2004.

49. "Researcher Thinks She Has Cancer Vaccine," Associated Press, January 25, 2005.

50. Debora MacKenzie, "Will Cancer Vaccine Get to All Women?" *New Scientist Magazine*, no. 2495 (April 18, 2005): 8. http://www.new scientist.com/article.ns?id=mg18624954.500&print.htm (accessed May 30, 2005).

51. American Life League, "Flawed Condom."

52. Patrick Goodenough, "Vaccine for Cancer-Causing Virus Could Spark Controversy," *Cybercast News Service*, April 28, 2005.

53. Ibid.

Chapter Five

1. Testimony presented by Dr. Ben-Maimon, president and chief operating officer of Barr Laboratories Research, a subsidiary of Barr Pharmaceuticals, before FDA advisory panels on making EC available over the counter, December 16, 2003. http://www.fda.gov/ohrms/dockets/ac/03/transcripts/4015T1.doc (accessed August 27, 2005); Charles Lockwood and Michael F. Greene, "Playing Politics with Women's Health: The FDA and Plan B," *Contemporary Ob/Gyn* (July 1, 2004).

2. Back Up Your Birth Control, "For the Press." http://www.backup yourbirthcontrol.org/press/index.htm (accessed July 4, 2005).

3. Center for Reproductive Rights, "Governments Worldwide Put Emergency Contraception into Women's Hands: A Global Review of Laws and Policies," briefing paper, September 2004, 3. http://www.reproductiverights.org/pdf/pub_bp_govtswwec.pdf.

4. Barbara Pillsbury, Francine Coeytaux, and Andrea Johnston, "From Secret to Shelf: How Collaboration Is Bringing Emergency Contraception to Women," Pacific Institute for Women's Health, 1999, 13. http://www.piwh.org/pdfs/ec_report.pdf.

5. U.S. Food and Drug Administration, "FDA Calls for Applications for Emergency Use of Oral Contraceptives," *FDA Medical Bulletin* 27, no. 1 (March 1997). http://www.fda.gov/medbull/mar97/notices.htm (accessed July 21, 2005).

6. "Emergency Contraception: FDA Approves 'Morning After' Pill," *American Political Network,* July 1, 1996.

7. Ralph T. King Jr., "Drugs: The Pill U.S. Drug Companies Dare Not Market," *Wall Street Journal,* June 26, 1998.

8. National Abortion Federation, "NAF Violence and Disruption Statistics: Incidents of Violence and Disruption against Abortion Providers in the U.S. and Canada," April 2005. http://www.prochoice.org/pubs_research/publications/downloads/about_abortion/violence_statistics.pdf.

9. King, "Drugs."

10. Ibid.

11. Rachel K. Jones, Jacqueline E. Darroch, and Stanley K. Henshaw, "Contraceptive Use among U.S. Women Having Abortions in 2000–2001," *Perspectives on Sexual and Reproductive Health* 34, no. 6 (November 1, 2002): 294–303.

12. Janelle Brown, "High Noon for the Morning After Pill," Salon.com, June 20, 2001.

13. Testimony presented by Dr. Ben-Maimon.

14. Back Up Your Birth Control, "For the Press."

15. Alan Guttmacher Institute, "Emergency Contraception: Increasing Public Awareness," *Issues in Brief,* 2005. http://www.guttmacher.org/pubs/ib_2-03-html (accessed July 4, 2005).

16. Barr Pharmaceuticals, Inc., "Barr Signs Letter of Intent to Acquire Plan B Emergency Contraceptive: Company Will Also Acquire Certain Assets and Liabilities of Women's Capital Corporation," press release, October 2, 2003. http://www.prnewswire.com/cgi-bin/stories.pl?ACCT=104&STORY=/www/story/10-02-2003/0002028423&EDATE=.

17. Joseph B. Stanford, "Sex, Naturally: Family Planning," *First Things: A Monthly Journal of Religion and Public Life* (November 1, 1999).

18. "Stanford's Giudice Selected to Chair Reproductive Health Drugs Committee." www.fdaadvisorycommittee.com/FDC/AdvisoryCommittee/Stories/ReproChair.htm (accessed July 8, 2005).

19. Marc Kaufman, "Memo May Have Swayed Plan B Ruling: FDA

Received 'Minority Report' from Conservatives on Panel," *Washington Post*, May 12, 2005.

20. Sarah Vos, "A Physician and a Lightning Rod: Anti-abortion Lexington Doctor, FDA Adviser, Stands Firm in Political Storm," *Lexington Herald Leader*, June 12, 2005.

21. Karen Tumulty, "Jesus and the FDA," *Time,* October 14, 2002.

22. Joni Westerhouse, "Macones Named Head of Obstetrics and Gynecology," Washington University in St. Louis Medical News Release, July 7, 2005. http://mednews.wustl.edu/news/page/normal/5468.html (accessed August 27, 2005).

23. "Charles J. Lockwood, M.D.," Department of Obstetrics, Gynecology, and Reproductive Sciences, Yale School of Medicine." http://info.med.yale.edu/obgyn/mfm/lockwood.html (accessed August 28, 2005).

24. Ayelish McGarvey, "Dr. Hager's Family Values," *Nation*, May 30, 2005. http://www.thenation.com/doc.mhtml?i=20050530&s=mcgarvey (accessed July 8, 2005).

25. Tumulty, "Jesus and the FDA."

26. Vos, "Physician and Lightning Rod."

27. Ibid.

28. Tumulty, "Jesus and the FDA."

29. U.S. Food and Drug Administration, Center for Drug Evaluation and Research, Nonprescription Drugs Advisory Committee (NDAC) in Joint Session with the Advisory Committee for Reproductive Health Drugs (ACRHD), Transcript of Meeting and Public Hearing Held Tuesday, December 16, 2003. http://www.fda.gov/ohrms/dockets/ac/03/transcripts/4015T1.htm (accessed July 5, 2005). Hereafter cited as FDA transcript.

30. Ibid.

31. William F. Colliton Jr., MD, "Birth Control Pill: Abortifacient and Contraceptive," American Association of Pro-Life Obstetricians and Gynecologists. http://www.aaplog.org/collition.htm (accessed July 7, 2005).

32. Hanna Klaus, "The Morning-After Pill: Another Step towards Depersonalization?" *Life and Learning* 7 (1997), University Faculty for Life. http://www.uffl.org/pastproceedings.htm (accessed July 7, 2005).

33. Judy Peres and Jeremy Manier, "'Morning After Pill' Not Abortion, Scientists Say," *Chicago Tribune*, June 20, 2005.

34. Ibid.

35. Jeffrey M. Drazen, MD, Michael F. Greene, MD, and Alastair J. J. Wood, MD, "The FDA, Politics, and Plan B," *New England Journal of Medicine* 350 (April 8, 2004): 1561–1562.

36. Testimony given by Dr. Ben-Maimon.

37. Reproductive Health and Research, "Emergency Contraception Pills: Medical Eligibility Criteria for Contraceptive Use," World Health Organization, Geneva, 3d ed., 2004. http://www.who.int/reproductive-health/publications/mec/6_ecps_july.pdf.

38. FDA transcript.

39. Ruth Rosen, "The Politics of Contraception," *San Francisco Chronicle*, May 13, 2004.

40. FDA transcript.

41. Ibid.

42. Jeffrey M. Drazen, MD, Michael F. Greene, MD, Alastair J. J. Wood, MD, "Correspondence," *New England Journal of Medicine* 350 (June 3, 2004): 2413–2414.

43. Ibid.

44. FDA transcript.

45. S. E. Anderson and A. Must, "Interpreting the Continued Decline in the Average Age at Menarche: Results from Two Nationally Representative Surveys of U.S. Girls Studied 10 Years Apart," *Journal of Pediatrics* 147 (forthcoming).

46. CDC, "Youth Risk Behavior Surveillance System, United States, 2003: Percentage of Students Who Had Sexual Intercourse for the First Time before Age 13," Youth Online: Comprehensive Results. http://www.cdc.gov/mmwr/preview/mmwrhtml/ss5302a1.htm.

47. Lockwood and Greene, "Playing Politics with Women's Health."

48. FDA transcript.

49. Drazen, Greene, and Wood, "The FDA, Politics, and Plan B."

50. Letter to President Bush from forty-nine congressmen urging the president to intervene in the FDA decision-making process, January 9,

2004. The names of the congressional members who signed the letter were confirmed by Paul Webster, legislative director for Congressman Dave Weldon, via e-mail correspondence, August 3, 2005, and compared to each legislator's voting record on abortion as provided by http://issues 2000.org (accessed August 8, 2005).

51. Ibid.

52. Tina R. Raine, MD, MPH, and others, "Direct Access to Emergency Contraception through Pharmacies and Effect on Unintended Pregnancy and STIs: A Randomized Controlled Trial," *Journal of the American Medical Association* 293 (January 5, 2005): 53–62.

53. Drazen, Greene, and Wood, "The FDA, Politics, and Plan B."

54. Drazen, Greene, and Wood, "Correspondence."

55. "Birth Control Pills: Contraceptive or Abortifacient?" Pro-Life Ob/Gyn's January 1998 statement, from Eternal Perspective Ministries. http://www.epm.org/articles/doctors.html (July 9, 2005).

56. Susan A. Crockett, MD, and others, "Hormonal Contraceptives: Controversies and Clarifications," American Association of Pro-Life Obstetricians and Gynecologists. http://www.aaplog.org/decook.htm (accessed July 9, 2005).

57. Sheryl Gay Stolberg, "After Impasse, F.D.A. May Fill Top Job," *New York Times*, September 25, 2002.

58. Kaufman, "Memo May Have Swayed Plan B Ruling."

59. Frank Lockwood, "Gynecologist Expects to Be Off Panel: *Nation* Article Puts Hager on Defensive," *Lexington Herald Leader*, May 13, 2005.

60. Union of Concerned Scientists, "Science Overruled on Emergency Contraception," from the July 2004 update to the group's February 2004 report "Scientific Integrity in Policymaking." http://www.ucsusa. org/global_environment/rsi/page.cfm?pageID=1443 (accessed August 20, 2005).

61. Rita Rubin, "Plan B Decision Called Political," *USA Today,* May 9, 2004.

62. Kaiser Daily Reproductive Health Report, "National Politics and Policy: FDA Official Rejected OTC Status for EC Plan B against Advice of Own Staff, Says Decision Not Based on Politics," May 10, 2004. http://

www.kaisernetwork.org/daily_reports/rep_index.cfm?hint=2&DR_ID=
23607 (accessed August 20, 2005).

63. Lockwood and Greene, "Playing Politics with Women's Health."

64. Sameh Fahmy, "Local Doctors Decry FDA Decision to Reject
Contraceptive Pill Advice," *Tennessean* (Nashville), May 13, 2004.

65. Stolberg, "After Impasse, F.D.A. May Fill Top Job."

66. "Plan B Should Be Over-the-Counter for Adolescents: Safety Data
Adequate," joint press release from the American Academy of Pediatrics
and the Society for Adolescent Medicine, May 27, 2004. http://www.aap.
org/advocacy/washing/Plan_B.htm (accessed August 20, 2005).

67. Union of Concerned Scientists, "Science Overruled on Emergency
Contraception."

68. Dawn Withers, "Contraceptive Fight Keeps FDA in Limbo: No
Permanent Chief of Agency in a Year," *Chicago Tribune*, May 4, 2005.

69. Union of Concerned Scientists, "Science Overruled on Emergency
Contraception."

70. Kaufman, "Memo May Have Swayed Plan B Ruling."

71. Reproductive Health Technologies Project, "Efforts to Bring EC
Over-the-Counter." http://www.rhtp.org/contraception/emergency/
efforts.asp (accessed July 8, 2005).

72. Lauran Neergaard, "FDA Delays Morning-After Pill's Nonprescription Sale," Associated Press, August 26, 2005.

73. Marc Kaufman, "FDA Rethinks Women's Chief," *Washington
Post*, September 20, 2005.

74. Marc Kaufman, "FDA: Plan B Sales Rejected against Advice: Official Denies That Politics Blocked Contraceptive's Over-the-Counter Status," *Washington Post*, May 8, 2004.

75. Ibid.

Chapter Six

1. "Maternal Mortality in 2000: Estimates Developed by WHO,
UNICEF, UNFPA," Annex Table G, Department of Reproductive Health

and Research, World Health Organization, Geneva, 2004. http://www.who.int/reproductive-health/publications/maternal_mortality_2000/mme.pdf (accessed October 20, 2005).

2. Ibid.

3. Save the Children, "Children Having Children, State of the World's Mothers, 2004," May 2004, 31. http://savethechildren.org/mothers report_2004/index.asp.

4. Campaign to End Fistula, "Fast Facts: Fistula and Reproductive Health," UNFPA. http://www.endfistula.org/fast_facts.htm (accessed July 27, 2005).

5. Save the Children, "Children Having Children," 31.

6. Ibid.

7. Adi Ignatius, "The People Who Influence Our Lives," *Time,* April 10, 2005.

8. Jeffrey Sachs, *The End of Poverty: Economic Possibilities for Our Time* (New York: Penguin Press, 2005), 65.

9. UNFPA, "UNFPA: United Nations Population Fund: Our Mission." http://www.unfpa.org/about/index.htm (accessed July 13, 2005).

10. UNFPA, "Frequently Asked Questions: Does UNFPA Promote Abortion?" http://www.unfpa.org/about/faqs.htm#abortion (accessed July 13, 2005).

11. "Hopkins Report: Contraceptive Funding Faces Crisis in Developing Countries," PR Newswire, June 6, 2002.

12. UNFPA, "Donor Pledges and Payments for 2004," Resources and Management. http://wwww.unfpa.org (accessed July 13, 2005).

13. Barbara Crossette, "34 Million Campaign Keeps Seeking New Friends," *Women's eNews*, November 17, 2003. http://www.34million friends.org/documents/news/wenews111703.htm (accessed July 27, 2005).

14. Dan Carpenter, "Politics and Poor Women," *Indianapolis Star*, July 23, 2003.

15. UNFPA, "Chapter IV: Gender Equality, Equity, and Empowerment of Women," summary of the ICPD Programme of Action. http://www.unfpa.org/icpd/summary.htm (accessed July 13, 2005).

16. UNFPA, "Introduction," summary of the ICPD Programme of Action. http://www.unfpa.org/icpd/summary.htm (accessed July 13, 2005).

17. UNFPA, "Chapter VIII: Health, Morbidity, and Mortality," summary of the ICPD Programme of Action. http://www.unfpa.org/icpd/summary.htm (accessed July 13, 2005).

18. CIA World Factbook. http://www.cia.gov/cia/publications/factbook/geos/ch.html (accessed July 25, 2005); "China Mission Report by UK MPs: 1st April–9th April 2002." http://www.planetwire.org/wrap.files.fcgi/2955_UK_report.htm (accessed July 22, 2005).

19. Amnesty International, "Frequently Asked Questions about Amnesty International's Campaign against Human Rights Violations in China." http://www.amnesty.org/ailib/intcam/china/china96/faq.htm (accessed July 13, 2005).

20. UNFPA, "UNFPA Welcomes U.S. Congress Support, Urges Administration to Release Funds," press release, January 23, 2004. http://www.unfpa.org/news/news.cfm?ID=411&Language=1 (accessed July 19, 2005).

21. China Population Information and Research Centre, "China/UNFPA: Reproductive Health/Family Planning: End of Project—Women Survey Report, Key Findings," Division of Social Statistics, University of Southampton, UK, February 2004. http://www.cpirc.org.cn/en/Report-CP4.pdf (accessed July 27, 2005), 42.

22. Catholics for a Free Choice, "The United Nations Population Fund in China: A Catalyst for Change, Report of an Interfaith Delegation to China," 2003, 6. http://www.catholicsforchoice.org/pdf/China%20Delegation%20Report%20Nov03.pdf.

23. Susan Cohen, "Bush Bars UNFPA Funding, Bucking Recommendation of Its Own Investigators," *Guttmacher Report on Public Policy* (October 2002). http://guttmacher.org/pubs/tgr/05/4/gr050413.html (accessed August 21, 2005).

24. Jodi Enda, "Lawmakers Take Aim at Decision to Cut Funding for Family Planning in China," Knight Ridder Washington Bureau, July 23, 2002.

25. Clifton Coles, "Women in War: Reproductive Health Is a Growing

Casualty of War and Other Crises; Demography," *Futurist*, November 1, 2004.

26. Susan A. Cohen, "U.S. Global Reproductive Health Policy: Isolationist Approach in an Interdependent World," *Guttmacher Report on Public Policy* (August 2004).

27. Planetwire.org, "Legislative Background: The Kemp-Kasten Amendment," Key Documents. http://www.planetwire.org/wrap/files/fcgi/2469_kempkasten.htm (accessed July 27, 2005).

28. Human Life International, "About Us." http://www.hli.org/about_us.html (accessed July 27, 2005).

29. "HLI's Population Group Gains Financial Independence—Funding Grows for PRI," press release, July 7, 2000, Catholic Online. http://www.catholic.org/prwire/headline.php?ID=123; Colby Anderson, "HLI's Population Group Gains Financial Independence-Funding Grows for PRI," Catholic Online.http://www.catholic.org/printer_friendly.php?id=123&section=Catholic+PRWire (accessed August 28, 2005).

30. Population Research Institute, 2002 IRS filing, Form 990 (most recent available), accessed through http://www.guidestar.org.

31. Population Research Institute, "PRI FAQs: What Is the Mission of PRI?" http://www.pop.org/main.cfm?EID=802 (accessed July 27, 2005).

32. Population Research Institute, "UNFPA, China, and Coercive Family Planning: An Investigative Report by Population Research Institute," December 21, 2001. http://www.pop.org/main.cfm?EID=312 (accessed June 28, 2005).

33. Ibid. (accessed April 29, 2005).

34. Ellen K. Johnson, "Six Billion's a Crowd?" *American Feminist* 9 (Spring 2002).

35. "Testimony of Dr. Nicolaas H. Biegman," U.S. Senate Foreign Relations Committee, Subcommittee on International Organizations and Terrorism, February 27, 2002. http://www.planetwire.org/wrap/files.fcgi/2346_Biegman.htm (accessed July 27, 2005).

36. Ibid.

37. Ibid.

38. Ibid.

39. Ibid.

40. Ibid.

41. Ibid.

42. Ibid.

43. U.S. Department of State, "Selection of U.S. Assessment Team to Visit China," press release, May 1, 2002. http://www.state.gov/r/pa/prs/ps/2002/9887.htm (accessed June 28, 2005).

44. Jodi Enda, "Small Advocacy Group Influences American Policy," Knight Ridder Newspapers, September 20, 2002.

45. U.S. Department of State, China UNFPA Independent Assessment Team, "Report of the China UN Populations Fund (UNFPA) Independent Assessment, Report of the China Independent Assessment Team," May 28, 2002. http://www.state.gov/g/prm/rls/rpt/2002/12122.htm (accessed June 28, 2005).

46. "China Mission Report by UK MPs."

47. Desikan Thirunarayanapuram, "Envoys to Probe Use of U.S. Funds for Forced Abortions," *Washington Times*, May 12, 2002.

48. "China Mission Report by UK MPs."

49. Michelle Goldberg, "The Zealots behind President Bush's U.N. Family Planning Sellout," Salon.com, June 13, 2002.

50. "Major Coalition Urges President Bush to Zero-Fund UNFPA," PR Newswire, June 20, 2002.

51. Ibid.; Population Research Institute, "U.S. Delegation to China: Another Whitewash in the Making," May 8, 2002. http://www.pop.org/main.cfm?EID=188 (accessed July 16, 2005).

52. Terry M. McNeal, "Downplaying Politics at the White House," *Washington Post*, July 24, 2002.

53. Jodi Enda, "Bush Poised to Cut Funding to UN Population Fund," Knight Ridder Washington Bureau, July 14, 2002.

54. Juliet Eilperin and Dana Milbank, "Bush May Cut U.N. Program's Funding: No Final Decision, but State Department Told to Plan Withholding Family Planning Aid," *Washington Post*, June 29, 2002.

55. Ben Barber, "Powell Enjoys Dissenting Adviser Role," *Washington Times*, August 5, 2002.

56. Matthew Lee, "U.S. Poised to Yank Funding from UN Population Fund over Abortion Claims," Agence France-Presse, July 14, 2002.

57. Ibid.

58. Michelle Goldberg, "A $34 Million 'Political Payoff,'" Salon.com, July 24, 2002.

59. Kaiser Daily Reproductive Health Report, "African Ambassadors to the United Nations Call on Bush Administration to Restore UNFPA Funding," August 12, 2002. http://www.kaisernetwork.org/daily_reports /rep_index.cfm?hint=2&DR_ID=12829 (accessed July 15, 2005); "African States Appeal to Powell on Population Fund," Reuters, August 9, 2002.

60. Kaiser Daily Reproductive Health Report, "Four Democratic Lawmakers Send Letter to Secretary of State Asking for Legal Explanation of UNFPA Funding Denial," June 21, 2004. http://www.kaisernetwork.org/ daily_repor/repndex.cfm?hint=2&DR_ID=24307 (accessed July 15, 2005).

61. Amor Safi, "Venezuela, North Korea, Iran, Russian, Israel/Palestinians, United Nations, Powell Meeting with Ambassador Bremer, Libya, China, Nepal, India, Vietnam," Federal Information and News Dispatch, Inc., State Department, August 27, 2003.

62. Rachel Swarns, "U.S. Cuts Off Financing for AIDS Program, Provoking Furor," *New York Times*, August 27, 2003.

63. Christopher Marquis, "U.S. Is Accused of Trying to Isolate UN Population Unit," *New York Times*, June 21, 2004.

64. Ibid.

65. Rick Mercier, "Davis Is Out Front on Family Planning 'Gag Rule,'" March 3, 2003. http://www.freelancestar.com.

66. Trudy Rubin, "Joining with Extremists: Bush Balked on Funds to UN Family-Planning Agency," *Philadelphia Inquirer*, July 26, 2002.

67. UNFPA, "Impact in Some Countries," Fact Sheet.

68. UNFPA, "34 Million Friends of UNFPA Campaign Hits $1 Mil-

lion Milestone," press release, May 1, 2003. http://www.unfpa.org/news/news.cfm?ID=312&Language=1 (accessed September 29, 2005).

69. "Hopkins Report: Contraceptive Funding Faces Crisis in Developing Countries," PR Newswire, June 6, 2002.

70. Deutsche Stiftung Weltbevoelkerung, "BMZ and DSW: US Decision to Withhold UNFPA Grant Will Bring Misery and Danger to Millions of Women," press release, July 24, 2002. http://www.planetwire.org/details/3013 (accessed July 27, 2005).

71. "European Commission News Release: Reproductive Health in Developing Countries: The Commission Moves to Fill the 'Decency Gap' with 32 Million [Euro] Package (July 24, 2002)," from Population Action International, "White House Denies Funding for United Nations Population Fund (UNFPA): Reactions from Around the World." http://www.populationaction.org/news/views/views_072502_UNFPA_reactions.htm (accessed August 21, 2005).

72. "Bush Stance on UN Body Deplored," *Irish Times*, September 16, 2004.

73. Kaiser Daily Reproductive Health Report, "Canadian Officials to Announce Increase Contribution to UNFPA," November 30, 2004. http://www.kaisernetwork.org/daily_reports/rep_index.cfm?hint=2&DR_ID=26949 (accessed July 15, 2005).

74. Kaiser Daily Reproductive Health Report, "European Union to Donate Funds to International Family Planning Programs to 'Fill the Gap' Left by Withdrawal of U.S. Funding," July 25, 2002. http://www.kaisernetwork.org/daily_reports/rep_index.cfm?hint=2&DR_ID=12518 (accessed July 15, 2005); personal correspondence with UNFPA spokesman Abubakar Dungus on the nature and structure of the EU's supplemental contribution.

75. American Life League, "Redirection of $34 Million from UNFPA to USAID a 'Stab in the Back.'" http://web.archive.org/web/20030618100512/http://www.all.org/news/020723.htm (accessed July 19, 2005).

76. Goldberg, "Zealots behind Bush's Sellout."

77. "UPI Focus: Kosovar Refugees Given Contraceptives," United Press International, May 19, 1999.

78. Goldberg, "Zealots behind Bush's Sellout."

79. "UN Population Fund Rejects False Allegations about Its Work in Afghanistan: Disinformation Endangers Women, United Nations Staff, and International Relief Workers, Says Agency," M2 Presswire, August 19, 2002.

80. Abubakar Dungus, "What is the composition of reproductive health kit? Is the kit on individual basis?" Description of reproductive health kits provided by UNFPA via e-mail correspondence to author, July 28, 2005.

81. PRI, "Backgrounder: Reasons Why the U.S. Should Not Be in the Business of Population Control," February 23, 1998. http://www.pop.org/main.cfm?Eid=317 (accessed September 27, 2005).

82. Thomas J. Euteneuer, "Special Report: Australia," Human Life International. http://www.hli.org/sr_9_2003.html#society (accessed September 27, 2005).

83. Steven Mosher, "Family Planners Eye Abortion Jihad in Iraq," Population Research Institute, March 18, 2003, vol. 5, no. 7. http://www.pop.org/main.cfm?EID=446 (accessed August 21, 2005).

84. Goldberg, "Zealots behind Bush's Sellout."

Chapter Seven

1. Naral Pro-Choice America, "Nationwide Trends, Key Findings: Who Decides? The Status of Women's Reproductive Rights in the United States," 2005. http://www.prochoiceamerica.org/yourstate/whodecides/trends/2005_key_findings.cfm (accessed August 5, 2005).

2. Center for Reproductive Rights, "What If *Roe* Fell: The State by State Consequences of Overturning *Roe v. Wade*," September 2004, 8. http://www.crlp.org/pdf/bo_whatifroefell.pdf.

3. Calculations based on data provided by the Alan Guttmacher Insti-

tute for each state's abortion statistics in 2000. http://www.guttmacher.org/statecenter/index.html (accessed August 5, 2005).

4. Center for Reproductive Rights, "What If *Roe* Fell."

5. Ibid.

6. Naral Pro-Choice America's Legal and Policy Research Department, "What Happens If *Roe* Is Overturned?" internal memorandum, January 13, 2005.

7. Position on abortion of state attorneys general gathered for Arizona, Georgia, Idaho, Illinois, Indiana, Iowa, Kansas, New Hampshire, Pennsylvania, Commonwealth of Puerto Rico, and the District of Columbia from Naral Pro-Choice America, "Who Decides? The Status of Women's Reproductive Rights in the United States, 2005." http://www.prochoiceamerica.org/yourstate/whodecides/index.cfm (accessed August 11, 2005).

8. Lawrence B. Finer and Stanley K. Henshaw, "Abortion Incidence and Services in the United States in 2000," *Perspectives on Sexual and Reproductive Health* 35 (2003): 6–15.

9. Ibid.

10. Tabulations made using state-specific abortion-provider numbers for the states expected to be outlawed or where the status is unclear from the Alan Guttmacher Institute data and the Center for Reproductive Rights' state lists from "What if *Roe* Fell?"

11. Leslie Reagan, *When Abortion Was a Crime: Women, Medicine, and Law in the United States, 1867–1973* (Berkeley and Los Angeles: University of California Press, 1997), 208.

12. Alan Guttmacher Institute, "Induced Abortion in the United States," *Fact in Brief* (May 2005).

13. Physicians for Reproductive Choice and Health and the Alan Guttmacher Institute, "Who Has Abortions? Economic Status," 2005.

14. Reagan, *When Abortion Was a Crime,* 198.

15. Ibid.

16. Ibid., 131, 120, 122, 123.

17. Ibid., 116.

18. National Conference of State Legislatures, "Fetal Homicide." http://www.ncsl.org/programs/health/fethom.htm (accessed August 8, 2005).

19. ACLU, "Arresting the Pregnancy Police: A Look at Fetal Protection Statutes and Wrongful Death Actions on Behalf of Fetuses," 1996. http://www.aclu.org/ReproductiveRights.cfm?ID=9055&c=144 (accessed July 26, 2005).

20. Debra Rosenberg, "*Roe*'s Army Reloads," *Newsweek*, August 8, 2005. Article cited poll of the Third Way Culture Project, the Gallup Organization, interview of 1,006 American adults by telephone, July 22–24.

21. Operation Rescue, "Announcing Operation Rescue's *Full-Scale Attack* on Legalized Baby-Killing in America . . . and How YOU Can Play *an Active Role* in the Life-or-Death Fight to Overturn *Roe v. Wade!*" http://www.operationrescue.org/?page_id=236 (accessed August 25, 2005).

22. "Biography of Supreme Court Justice John Paul Stevens," Naral Pro-Choice America. http://www.prochoiceamerica.org/facts/stevensbio.cfm (accessed October 20, 2005).

23. Naral Pro-Choice America, "Bush's War on the Right to Choose and the Right to Privacy by the Numbers." http://www.prochoiceamerica.org/facts/loader.cfm?url=/commonspot/security/getfile.cfm&PageID=16580 (accessed August 3, 2005).

24. Charles Hurt, "Democrats Seek View on *Roe* from Roberts," *Washington Times*, July 28, 2005.

25. United States District Court for the Northern District of Texas, *Roe v. Wade*, (No. 70–18), 314 F.Supp. 1217, affirmed in part and reversed in part. http://www.law.cornell.edu/supct/html/historics/USSC_CR_0410_0113_ZD.html (accessed August 17, 2005).

26. "Impact: At Home Abortion Leads to Life in Prison," *The O'Reilly Factor*, June 8, 2005, interview with boy's attorney.

27. Chad Halcom, "Fathers in Teen Abortion Case Discuss Communicating with Their Children," *Macomb Daily*, January 7, 2005.

28. Edward L. Cardenas and George Hunter, "Boy Faces Felony in Baseball Bat Abortion: Law Won't Allow Macomb Teen Girl to Be Charged in Helping End Her Pregnancy," *Detroit News*, January 5, 2005.

29. Kaiser Daily Reproductive Health, "Boy Charged with Felony for Helping Girlfriend End Pregnancy: Michigan Law Prevents Legal Action against Girl," January 6, 2005. http://www.kaisernetwork.org/daily_reports.cfm?DR_ID=27498&dr_cat=2 (accessed February 15, 2005).

30. Edward L. Cardenas, "Dads Blast Prosecutor in Fetus Case: The Father of the Boy Accused of Causing the Miscarriage Says He Was Charged to Boost the Official's Career," *Detroit News*, January 7, 2005.

31. Transcript, "Interview with Eric Smith, Miranda Massie," *Fox on the Record with Greta Van Susteren*, January 17, 2005.

32. Edward Cardenas, "Teen Must Serve Pro-Life Center: Judge's Order for Boy Convicted of Hitting Girlfriend with a Bat to End Pregnancy Prompts Objections," *Detroit News*, September 30, 2005.

33. Amber Hunt Martin, "Legislator Seeks Change in Prenatal Protection Act: Women Would Face Criminal Charges, Too," *Detroit Free Press*, February 7, 2005.

34. "Prenatal Protection Act Likely Set for Change," *Jacobs Report*, newsletter of Michigan State senator Gilda Z. Jacobs, January 7, 2005. http://www.senate.michigan.gov/dem/gildajacobs/weeklyreports/010705.pdf (accessed August 10, 2005).

35. Rick Brundrett, "Woman's Abortion Is Unique S.C. Case," *Columbia (SC) State*, May 1, 2005.

36. Ibid.

37. Naral Pro-Choice America e-mail correspondence to author, August 26, 2005.

38. Naral Pro-Choice America, "Mandatory Parental Consent and Notice Laws Burden the Freedom to Choose," December 27, 2004. http://www.naral.org/facts/loader.cfm?url=/commonspot/security/getfile.cfm&PageID=2058 (accessed October 20, 2005).

39. Planned Parenthood Federation of America, "Supreme Court to Hear Case Challenging Access to Abortion: During Time of Heated Judicial Rhetoric, *Ayotte v. Planned Parenthood* to Be Heard by High Court," press release, May 23, 2005. http://www.plannedparenthood.org/pp2/portal/media/pressreleases/pr-050523-supreme-court.xml.

40. Boulder Abortion Clinic, "Fetal Anomaly." http://www.gynpages.com/boulder/fetalanomaly.html (accessed August 28, 2005).

41. Kaiser Daily Reproductive Health Report, "Military Not Required to Pay for Abortion of Nonviable Fetus under Federal Law, 9th Circuit Court of Appeals Rules," August 19, 2005. http://www.kaisernetwork.org/daily_reports/rep_index.cfm?hint=2&DR_ID=32108 (accessed August 19, 2005).

42. United States Supreme Court, *Griswold v. Connecticut* (No. 496), 151 Conn. 544, 200 A.2d 479, reversed. http://www.law.cornell.edu/supct/html/historics/USSC_CR_0381_0479_ZO.html.

43. "Thomas, J., Dissenting, Supreme Court of the United States, no. 02—102, John Geddes Lawrence and Tyron Garner, Petitioners *V.* Texas, on Writ of Certiorari to the Court of Appeals of Texas, Fourteenth District, June 26, 2003." http://www.law.cornell.edu/supct/html/02-102.ZD1.html (accessed August 15, 2005). Brackets included in quote are Justice Thomas's.

44. David Garrow, "The Tragedy of William O. Douglas," *Nation*, April 14, 2003. http://ssl.thenation.com/doc.mhtml?i=20030414&c=3&s=garrow (accessed August 18, 2005).

45. People for the American Way, "Courting Disaster 2005: Privacy and Reproductive Freedom." http://www.pfaw.org/pfaw/general/default.aspx?oid=11124 (accessed August 15, 2005).

46. People for the American Way, "40th Anniversary of *Griswold* Highlights Threat to Privacy Rights from Future Supreme Court Nominees," press release, June 7, 2005. http://www.pfaw.org/pfaw/general/default.aspx?oID=18876 (accessed August 15, 2005).

47. Concerned Women for America, "Life, Lies, and Hard Cases." http://www.cwfa.org/articledisplay.asp?id=3110&department=CWA&categoryid=life (accessed August 15, 2005); Dr. Robert P. George, "Judicial Activism and the Constitution: Solving a Growing Crisis," Family Research Council, August 15, 2005. http://www.frc.org/get.cfm?i=IS05D01&v=PRINT (accessed August 15, 2005).

48. "Sen. Rick Santorum's Comments on Homosexuality in an AP Interview," Associated Press State and Local Wire, April 23, 2003.

49. Rachel Benson Gold, "The Implications of Defining When a Woman Is Pregnant," *Guttmacher Report on Public Policy* (May 2005).

50. "Senators Question Rove's Role: Supreme Court Nomination Fight—Did Bush Adviser Give 'Back-Room Assurances'?" *Seattle Times,* October 10, 2005.

51. Maura Reynolds and Edwin Chen, "Interpretations Differ after Talks with Miers: Specter Reports That the High Court Nominee Believes in the Right to Privacy, but Later the White House Says He Misunderstood Her," *Los Angeles Times,* October 18, 2005.

52. Adam Liptak, "In Abortion Rulings, Idea of Marriage Is Pivotal," *New York Times,* November 2, 2005.

53. O'Connor opinion, *"Planned Parenthood of Southeastern Pa. v. Casey* (91-744), 505 U.S. 833 (1992)." http://straylight.law.cornell.edu/supct/html/91-744.ZO.html (accessed November 5, 2005).

Acknowledgments

WRITING A BOOK is a lot like being pregnant. And if this book was a pregnancy, it was unintended, high-risk, with many complications, but wanted. And just like any pregnancy, to get through it you rely on the help of many people: loved ones, colleagues, and specialists.

I consulted with many experts to whom I am grateful for insight and expert guidance, including Louise Melling, Eve Gartner, Priscilla Smith, Abubkar Dungus, Stirling Scruggs, Donna Crane, Myra Batchelder, Ellen Chesler, Dr. David Grimes, James Trussell, Jay Belsky, Claire Keyes, Robin Rothrock, Dr. William Harrison, Chris Charbonneau, Rebecca Wind, Deborah Friedman, Susan Yanow, and Carol Petratis. I am also deeply grateful to my colleagues at Naral Pro-Choice New York, and particularly to Kelli Conlin and Bob Jaffe, for their constant support in completing the book. During any leave of absence, you rely on colleagues to shoulder the load you can't. Few workplaces are as generous as mine and this is because people there recognize that life is full of surprises, important ones, and the workplace should accommodate them. I am indebted to Barbara Shack, Eric Alterman, Jeanne McMahon, Ed Liebman, Kim Gerstman, Mary Alice Carr, Rebecca Raible, Sara Weinstein, Christina Tenuta, Andrew Stern, Pauline DeMairo, Destiny Lopez and Nika Charity for their support. Erin Mears and

Pam Zimmerman were eager and enthusiastic interns able to unearth difficult to find legal passages and statutes.

My editors, Jo Ann Miller, Ellen Garrison and Megan Hustad, like good doctors, monitored my progress throughout and diagnosed problems early, ensuring safe passage through the most complicated periods. I am thankful to have worked with my publicist Holly Bemiss, and a group of talented publishing pros: Jamie Brickhouse, and John Sherer, Marty Gosser, Matty Goldberg, Christine Marra, Kevin Goering, Annette Wenda, and Donna Riggs. My agent, Jane Gelfman, was an ongoing source of encouragement. Andrew Sharp, Laura Nolan, Betsy McCaughey, Scott Pellegrino, Ilan Sandberg, Karla Silverman and Peter Mendelsund were reliable and bighearted suppliers of sound advice. And Liz Maguire was a friend who, with signature humor and prescience, convinced me to do this in the first place.

My greatest needs in the bookmaking process—and what no person should try alone—is the final delivery. Emily Alexander helped me through this difficult phase. She was like a midwife (and a doula too).

My mother, as great mothers do, listened (and shared the pain) through all the trying phases; she was the one in whom I could confide at my deepest moments of doubt.

But it is my husband, Steve, who had played the pivotal part in helping nurture this work. I could not have done it without him, nor would I have wanted to attempt it. He was there from inception to completion.

An unforgiving book deadline consumes a whole family, and more. My new son's wonderful nanny Nicole helped him at all turns—and helped keep my anxiety at a controllable level. Working from home allowed for cherished surprises, such as the chance to abandon the bedroom/office to monitor my son's first steps, or respond to his tiny knock on the door summoning me to play hooky for a squeal-filled half hour. His language was developing as I wrote and he learned a few interesting phrases, like "mommy work" and "me-mail." Now my home office will resume its primary role as bedroom. The door will remain open and when my son next pokes in his head I hope together we can figure out an answer to that age old question, Who can jump higher on the mattress?

Index